The State of Food Insecurity in the World

Meeting the 2015 international hunger targets: taking stock of uneven progress

FOOD AND AGRICULTURE ORGANIZATION OF THE UNITED NATIONS

Rome, 2015

Required citation:
FAO, IFAD and WFP. 2015. *The State of Food Insecurity in the World 2015.*
Meeting the 2015 international hunger targets: taking stock of uneven progress.
Rome, FAO.

ISBN 978-92-5-108800-5

CONTENTS

This year's annual *State of Food Insecurity in the World* report takes stock of progress made towards achieving the internationally established hunger targets, and reflects on what needs to be done, as we transition to the new post-2015 Sustainable Development Agenda.

United Nations member states have made two major commitments to tackle world hunger. The first was at the World Food Summit (WFS), in Rome in 1996, when 182 governments committed *"... to eradicate hunger in all countries, with an immediate view to reducing the number of undernourished people to half their present level no later than 2015"*. The second was the formulation of the First Millennium Development Goal (MDG 1), established in 2000 by the United Nations members, which includes among its targets *"cutting by half the proportion of people who suffer from hunger by 2015"*.

In this report, we review progress made since 1990 for every country and region as well as for the world as a whole. First, the good news: overall, the commitment to halve the percentage of hungry people, that is, to reach the MDG 1c target, has been almost met at the global level. More importantly, 72 of the 129 countries monitored for progress have reached the MDG target, 29 of which have also reached the more ambitious WFS goal by at least halving the number of undernourished people in their populations.

Marked differences in progress occur not only among individual countries, but also across regions and subregions. The prevalence of hunger has been reduced rapidly in Central, Eastern and South-Eastern Asia as well as in Latin America; in Northern Africa, a low level has been maintained throughout the MDG and WFS monitoring periods. Other regions, including the Caribbean, Oceania and Western Asia, saw some overall progress, but at a slower pace. In two regions, Southern Asia and sub-Saharan Africa, progress has been slow overall, despite many success stories at country and subregional levels. In many countries that have achieved modest progress, factors such as war, civil unrest and the displacement of refugees have often frustrated efforts to reduce hunger, sometimes even raising the ranks of the hungry.

Progress towards the MDG 1c target, however, is assessed not only by measuring undernourishment, or hunger, but also by a second indicator – the prevalence of underweight children under five years of age. Progress for the two indicators was similar, but slightly faster in the case of undernourishment. While both indicators have moved in parallel for the world as a whole, they diverge significantly at the regional level owing to the different determinants of child underweight.

Overall progress notwithstanding, hunger remains an everyday challenge for almost 795 million people worldwide, including 780 million in the developing regions. Hence, hunger eradication should remain a key commitment of decision-makers at all levels.

In this year's *State of Food Insecurity of the World*, we not only estimate the progress already achieved, but also identify remaining problems, and offer recommendations for how these can be addressed. In a nutshell, there is no "one-size-fits-all" solution. Interventions must be tailored to conditions, including food availability and access, as well as longer-term development prospects. Approaches need to be appropriate and comprehensive, with the requisite political commitment to secure success.

Much work, therefore, remains to be done to eradicate hunger and achieve food security across all its dimensions. This report identifies key factors that have determined success to date in reaching the MDG 1c hunger target, and provides guidance on which policies should be emphasized in the future.

Inclusive growth provides opportunities for those with meagre assets and skills, and improves the livelihoods and incomes of the poor, especially in agriculture. It is therefore among the most effective tools for fighting hunger and food insecurity, and for attaining sustainable progress. Enhancing the productivity of resources held by smallholder family farmers, fisherfolk and forest communities, and promoting their rural economic integration through well-functioning markets, are essential elements of inclusive growth.

Social protection contributes directly to the reduction of hunger and malnutrition. By increasing human capacities and promoting income security, it fosters local economic development and the ability of the poor to secure decent employment and thus partake of economic growth. There are many "win-win" situations to be found linking family farming and social protection. They include institutional purchases from local farmers to supply school meals and government programmes, and cash transfers or cash-for-work programmes that allow communities to buy locally produced food.

During protracted crises, due to conflicts and natural disasters, food insecurity and malnutrition loom even larger. These challenges call for strong political commitment and effective actions.

More generally, progress in the fight against food insecurity requires coordinated and complementary responses from all stakeholders. As heads of the three Rome-based food and agriculture agencies, we have been and will continue to be at the forefront of these efforts, working together to support member states, their organizations and other stakeholders to overcome hunger and malnutrition.

Major new commitments to hunger reduction have recently been taken at the regional level – the Hunger-Free Latin America and the Caribbean Initiative, Africa's Renewed Partnership to End Hunger by 2025, the Zero Hunger Initiative for West Africa, the Asia-Pacific Zero Hunger Challenge, and pilot initiatives of Bangladesh, the Lao People's Democratic Republic, Myanmar, Nepal and Timor-Leste, among other countries. Further initiatives are in the making to eradicate hunger by the year 2025 or 2030.

These efforts deserve and have our unequivocal support to strengthen national capacities and capabilities to successfully develop and deliver the needed programmes. Advances since 1990 show that making hunger, food insecurity and malnutrition history is possible. They also show that there is a lot of work ahead if we are to transform that vision into reality. Political commitment, partnership, adequate funding and comprehensive actions are key elements of this effort, of which we are active partners.

As dynamic members of the United Nations system, we shall support national and other efforts to make hunger and malnutrition history through the Zero Hunger Challenge, the 2014 Rome Declaration on Nutrition and the post-2015 Sustainable Development Agenda.

José Graziano da Silva
FAO Director-General

Kanayo F. Nwanze
IFAD President

Ertharin Cousin
WFP Executive Director

ACKNOWLEDGEMENTS

The State of Food Insecurity in the World has been jointly prepared by the Food and Agriculture Organization of the United Nations (FAO), the International Fund for Agricultural Development (IFAD) and the World Food Programme (WFP).

Technical coordination of the publication was carried out, under the overall leadership of Jomo Kwame Sundaram, by Pietro Gennari, with the support of Kostas Stamoulis of the FAO Economic and Social Development Department (ES). Piero Conforti, George Rapsomanikis and Josef Schmidhuber, of FAO, Rui Benfica, of IFAD, and Arif Husain of WFP served as technical editors. Valuable comments and final approval of the report were provided by the executive heads of the three Rome-based agencies and their offices, with Coumba Dieng Sow and Lucas Tavares (FAO).

The section on *Undernourishment around the world in 2015* was drafted with technical inputs from Filippo Gheri, Erdgin Mane, Nathalie Troubat and Nathan Wanner, and the Food Security and Social Statistics team of the FAO Statistics Division (ESS). Supporting data were provided by Mariana Campeanu, Tomasz Filipczuk, Nicolas Sakoff, Salar Tayyib and the Food Balance Sheets team of the same Division.

The section on *Inside the hunger target: comparing trends in undernourishment and underweight in children* was prepared with substantive inputs from Chiara Brunelli and the Food Security and Social Statistics team of the FAO Statistics Division (ESS).

The section on *Food security and nutrition: the drivers of change* was prepared with inputs from Federica Alfani, Lavinia Antonacci, Romina Cavatassi, Ben Davis, Julius Jackson, Panagiotis Karfakis, Leslie Lipper, Luca Russo and Elisa Scambelloni of the FAO Agricultural Development Economics Division (ESA); Ekaterina Krivonos and Jamie Morrison of the FAO Trade and Markets Division (EST); Meshack Malo, of the FAO Office of the Deputy Director-General Natural Resources; Francesco Pierri of the FAO Office for Partnerships, Advocacy and Capacity Development; Constanza Di Nucci (IFAD); and Niels Balzer, Kimberly Deni, Paul Howe, Michelle Lacey and John McHarris (WFP).

Filippo Gheri was responsible for preparing Annex 1 and the related data processing. Nathan Wanner, with key technical contributions from Carlo Cafiero, prepared Annex 2.

Valuable comments and suggestions were provided by Raul Benitez, Eduardo Rojas Briales, Gustavo Merino Juárez, Arni Mathiesen, Eugenia Serova and Rob Vos (FAO); Karim Hussein and Edward Heinemann (IFAD); and Richard Choularton and Sarah Kohnstamm (WFP).

Michelle Kendrick (ES) coordinated the editorial, graphics, layout and publishing process. Graphic design and layout services were provided by Flora Dicarlo. Production of the translated editions was coordinated by the FAO Library and Publications Branch of the Office for Corporate Communication. Translation and printing services were coordinated by the Meeting Programming and Documentation Service of the FAO Conference, Council and Protocol Affairs Division.

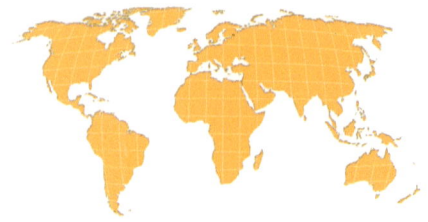

Undernourishment around the world in 2015

The global trends

Progress continues in the fight against hunger, yet an unacceptably large number of people still lack the food they need for an active and healthy life. The latest available estimates indicate that about 795 million people in the world – just over one in nine – were undernourished in 2014–16 (Table 1). The share of undernourished people in the population, or the prevalence of undernourishment (PoU),[1] has decreased from 18.6 percent in 1990–92 to 10.9 percent in 2014–16, reflecting fewer undernourished people in a growing global population. Since 1990–92, the number of undernourished people has declined by 216 million globally, a reduction of 21.4 percent, notwithstanding a 1.9 billion

TABLE **1**

Undernourishment around the world, 1990–92 to 2014–16

| | Number of undernourished (millions) and prevalence (%) of undernourishment | | | | | | | | | |
| | **1990–92** | | **2000–02** | | **2005–07** | | **2010–12** | | **2014–16*** | |
	No.	**%**	**No.**	**%**	**No.**	**%**	**No.**	**%**	**No.**	**%**
WORLD	1 010.6	18.6	929.6	14.9	942.3	14.3	820.7	11.8	794.6	10.9
DEVELOPED REGIONS	20.0	<5.0	21.2	<5.0	15.4	<5.0	15.7	<5.0	14.7	<5.0
DEVELOPING REGIONS	990.7	23.3	908.4	18.2	926.9	17.3	805.0	14.1	779.9	12.9
Africa	181.7	27.6	210.2	25.4	213.0	22.7	218.5	20.7	232.5	20.0
Northern Africa	6.0	<5.0	6.6	<5.0	7.0	<5.0	5.1	<5.0	4.3	<5.0
Sub-Saharan Africa	175.7	33.2	203.6	30.0	206.0	26.5	205.7	24.1	220.0	23.2
Eastern Africa	103.9	47.2	121.6	43.1	122.5	37.8	118.7	33.7	124.2	31.5
Middle Africa	24.2	33.5	42.4	44.2	47.7	43.0	53.0	41.5	58.9	41.3
Southern Africa	3.1	7.2	3.7	7.1	3.5	6.2	3.6	6.1	3.2	5.2
Western Africa	44.6	24.2	35.9	15.0	32.3	11.8	30.4	9.7	33.7	9.6
Asia	741.9	23.6	636.5	17.6	665.5	17.3	546.9	13.5	511.7	12.1
Caucasus and Central Asia	9.6	14.1	10.9	15.3	8.4	11.3	7.1	8.9	5.8	7.0
Eastern Asia	295.4	23.2	221.7	16.0	217.6	15.2	174.7	11.8	145.1	9.6
South-Eastern Asia	137.5	30.6	117.6	22.3	103.2	18.3	72.5	12.1	60.5	9.6
Southern Asia	291.2	23.9	272.3	18.5	319.1	20.1	274.2	16.1	281.4	15.7
Western Asia	8.2	6.4	14.0	8.6	17.2	9.3	18.4	8.8	18.9	8.4
Latin America and the Caribbean	66.1	14.7	60.4	11.4	47.1	8.4	38.3	6.4	34.3	5.5
Caribbean	8.1	27.0	8.2	24.4	8.3	23.5	7.3	19.8	7.5	19.8
Latin America	58.0	13.9	52.1	10.5	38.8	7.3	31.0	5.5	26.8	<5.0
Central America	12.6	10.7	11.8	8.3	11.6	7.6	11.3	6.9	11.4	6.6
South America	45.4	15.1	40.3	11.4	27.2	7.2	ns	<5.0	ns	<5.0
Oceania	1.0	15.7	1.3	16.5	1.3	15.4	1.3	13.5	1.4	14.2

*Data for 2014–16 refer to provisional estimates.
Source: FAO.

increase in total population over the same period. The vast majority of the hungry live in the developing regions,[2] where an estimated 780 million people were undernourished in 2014–16 (Table 1). The PoU, standing at 12.9 percent in 2014–16, has fallen by 44.5 percent since 1990–92.

Changes in large populous countries, notably China and India, play a large part in explaining the overall hunger reduction trends in the developing regions.[3] Rapid progress was achieved during the 1990s, when the developing regions as a whole experienced a steady decline in both the number of undernourished and the PoU (Figure 1). This was followed by a slowdown in the PoU in the early 2000s before a renewed acceleration in the latter part of the decade, with the PoU falling from 17.3 percent in 2005–07 to 14.1 percent in 2010–12. Estimates for the most recent period, partly based on projections, have again seen a phase of slower progress, with the PoU declining to 12.9 percent by 2014–16.

■ Measuring global progress against targets

The year 2015 marks the end of the monitoring period for the two internationally agreed targets for hunger reduction. The first is the World Food Summit (WFS) goal. At the WFS, held in Rome in 1996, representatives of 182 governments pledged "... *to eradicate hunger in all countries, with an immediate view to reducing the number of undernourished people to half their present level no later than 2015*".[4] The second is the Millennium Development Goal 1 (MDG 1) hunger target. In 2000, 189 nations pledged to free people from multiple deprivations, recognizing that every individual has the right to dignity, freedom, equality and a basic standard of living that includes freedom from hunger and violence. This pledge led to the formulation of eight Millennium Development Goals (MDGs) in 2001. The MDGs were then made operational by the establishment of targets and indicators to track progress, at national and global levels, over a reference period of 25 years, from 1990 to 2015. The first MDG, or MDG 1, includes three distinct targets: halving global poverty, achieving full and productive employment and decent work for all, and cutting by half the proportion of people who suffer from hunger[5] by 2015. FAO has monitored progress towards the WFS and the MDG 1c hunger targets, using the three-year period 1990–92 as the starting point.

The latest PoU estimates suggest that the developing regions as a whole have almost reached the MDG 1c hunger target. The estimated reduction in 2014–16 is less than one percentage point away from that required to reach the target by 2015 (Figure 1).[6] Given this small difference, and allowing for a margin of reliability of the background data used to estimate undernourishment, the target can be considered as having been achieved. However, as indicated in the 2013 and 2014 editions of this report, meeting the target exactly would have required accelerated progress in recent years. Despite significant progress in many countries,

the needed acceleration does not seem to have materialized in the developing regions as a whole.

The other target, set by the WFS in 1996, has been missed by a large margin. Current estimates peg the number of undernourished people in 1990–92 at a little less than a billion in the developing regions. Meeting the WFS goal would have required bringing this number down to about 515 million, that is, some 265 million fewer than the current estimate for 2014–16 (Table 1). However, considering that the population has grown by 1.9 billion since 1990–92, about two billion people have been freed from a likely state of hunger over the past 25 years.

Significant progress in fighting hunger over the past decade should be viewed against the backdrop of a challenging global environment: volatile commodity prices, overall higher food and energy prices, rising unemployment and underemployment rates and, above all, the global economic recessions that occurred in the late 1990s and again after 2008. Increasingly frequent extreme weather events and natural disasters have taken a huge toll in terms of human lives and economic damage, hampering efforts to enhance food security. Political instability and civil strife have added to this picture, bringing the number of displaced persons globally to the highest level since the Second World War. These developments have taken their toll on food security in some of the most vulnerable countries, particularly

FIGURE **1**

The trajectory of undernourishment in developing regions: actual and projected progress towards the MDG and WFS targets

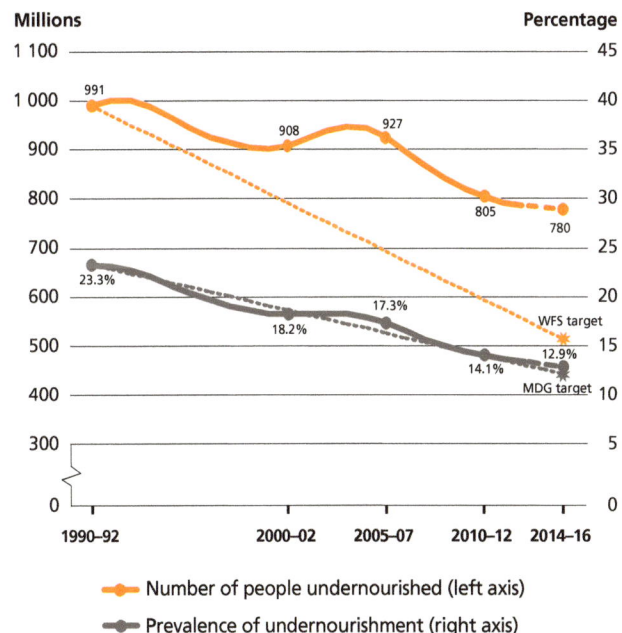

Note: Data for 2014–16 refer to provisional estimates.
Source: FAO.

in sub-Saharan Africa, while other regions such as Eastern and South-Eastern Asia, have remained unaffected or have been able to minimize the adverse impacts.

The changing global economic environment has challenged traditional approaches to addressing hunger. Social safety nets and other measures that provide targeted assistance to the most vulnerable population groups have received growing attention. The importance of such targeted measures, when combined with long-term and structural interventions, lies in their ability to lead to a virtuous circle of better nutrition and higher labour productivity. Direct interventions are most effective when they target the most vulnerable populations and address their specific needs,

improving the quality of their diet. Even where policies have been successful in addressing large food-energy deficits, dietary quality remains a concern. Southern Asia and sub-Saharan Africa remain particularly exposed to what has become known as "hidden hunger" – the lack of, or inadequate, intake of micronutrients, resulting in different types of malnutrition, such as iron-deficiency anaemia and vitamin A deficiency.

How the challenges posed by the global economic environment affect individual regions, and the policies adopted to counteract them, are discussed in greater detail in the third section of this report, "Food security and nutrition: the drivers of change (see pp. 26–42)".

Wide differences persist among regions

Progress towards improved food security continues to be uneven across regions. Some regions have made remarkably rapid progress in reducing hunger, notably the Caucasus and Central Asia, Eastern Asia, Latin America and Northern Africa. Others, including the Caribbean, Oceania and Western Asia, have also reduced their PoU, but at a slower pace. Progress has also been uneven within these regions, leaving significant pockets of food insecurity in a number of

countries. In two regions, Southern Asia and sub-Saharan Africa, progress has been slow overall. While some countries report successes in reducing hunger, undernourishment and other forms of malnutrition remain at overall high levels in these regions.

The different rates of progress across regions have brought about changes in the regional distribution of hunger since the early 1990s (Figure 2). Southern Asia and

FIGURE **2**

The changing distribution of hunger in the world: numbers and shares of undernourished people by region, 1990–92 and 2014–16

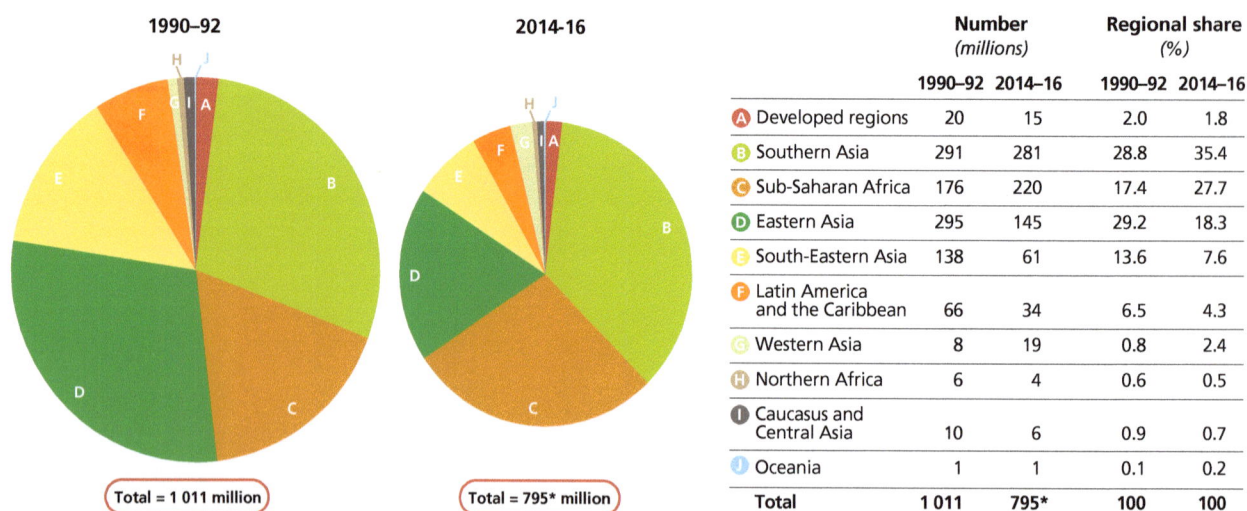

		Number (millions)		Regional share (%)	
		1990–92	2014–16	1990–92	2014–16
A	Developed regions	20	15	2.0	1.8
B	Southern Asia	291	281	28.8	35.4
C	Sub-Saharan Africa	176	220	17.4	27.7
D	Eastern Asia	295	145	29.2	18.3
E	South-Eastern Asia	138	61	13.6	7.6
F	Latin America and the Caribbean	66	34	6.5	4.3
G	Western Asia	8	19	0.8	2.4
H	Northern Africa	6	4	0.6	0.5
I	Caucasus and Central Asia	10	6	0.9	0.7
J	Oceania	1	1	0.1	0.2
	Total	**1 011**	**795***	**100**	**100**

1990–92   Total = 1 011 million

2014-16   Total = 795* million

Notes: The areas of the pie charts are proportional to the total number of undernourished in each period. Data for 2014–16 refer to provisional estimates. All figures are rounded.
*Includes data for Sudan, which are not included in the figure for sub-Saharan Africa, following the partition of the country when South Sudan became an independent state in 2011.
Source: FAO.

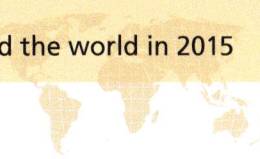

sub-Saharan Africa now account for substantially larger shares of global undernourishment.[7] The shares for Oceania and Western Asia also rose, albeit by much smaller margins and from relatively low levels. In tandem, faster-than-average progress in Eastern Asia and Latin America and the Caribbean means that these regions now account for much smaller shares of global undernourishment.

Progress towards the international hunger targets

Figure 3 shows how the various developing regions fare with respect to these targets. The estimates suggest that Africa as a whole, and sub-Saharan Africa in particular, will not achieve the MDG 1c target. Northern Africa, by contrast, has reached the target.[8] The more ambitious WFS goal, however, appears to be out of reach for Africa as a whole, as well as for all its subregions. Asia as a region has already achieved

the MDG 1c hunger target, but would need a further reduction of about 140 million undernourished people to reach the WFS goal – an achievement that is unlikely to materialize in the near future. Latin America and the Caribbean, considered together, have achieved both the MDG 1c hunger target and the WFS goal in 2014–16. Finally, Oceania has reached neither the MDG 1c hunger target nor the WFS goal.

Some countries have met both international targets. Based on the latest estimates, a total of 72 developing countries have achieved the MDG 1c hunger target by 2014–16 (Tables 2 and 3).[9] Of these, 29 countries have also reached the WFS goal. Another 31 developing countries have reached only the MDG 1c hunger target, either by reducing the PoU by 50 percent or more, or by bringing it below 5 percent. Finally, a third group of 12 countries is also categorized alongside those that have reached the MDG 1c hunger target, as they have maintained their PoU close to or below 5 percent since 1990–92.

FIGURE **3**

Regions differ markedly in progress towards achieving the MDG and WFS hunger targets

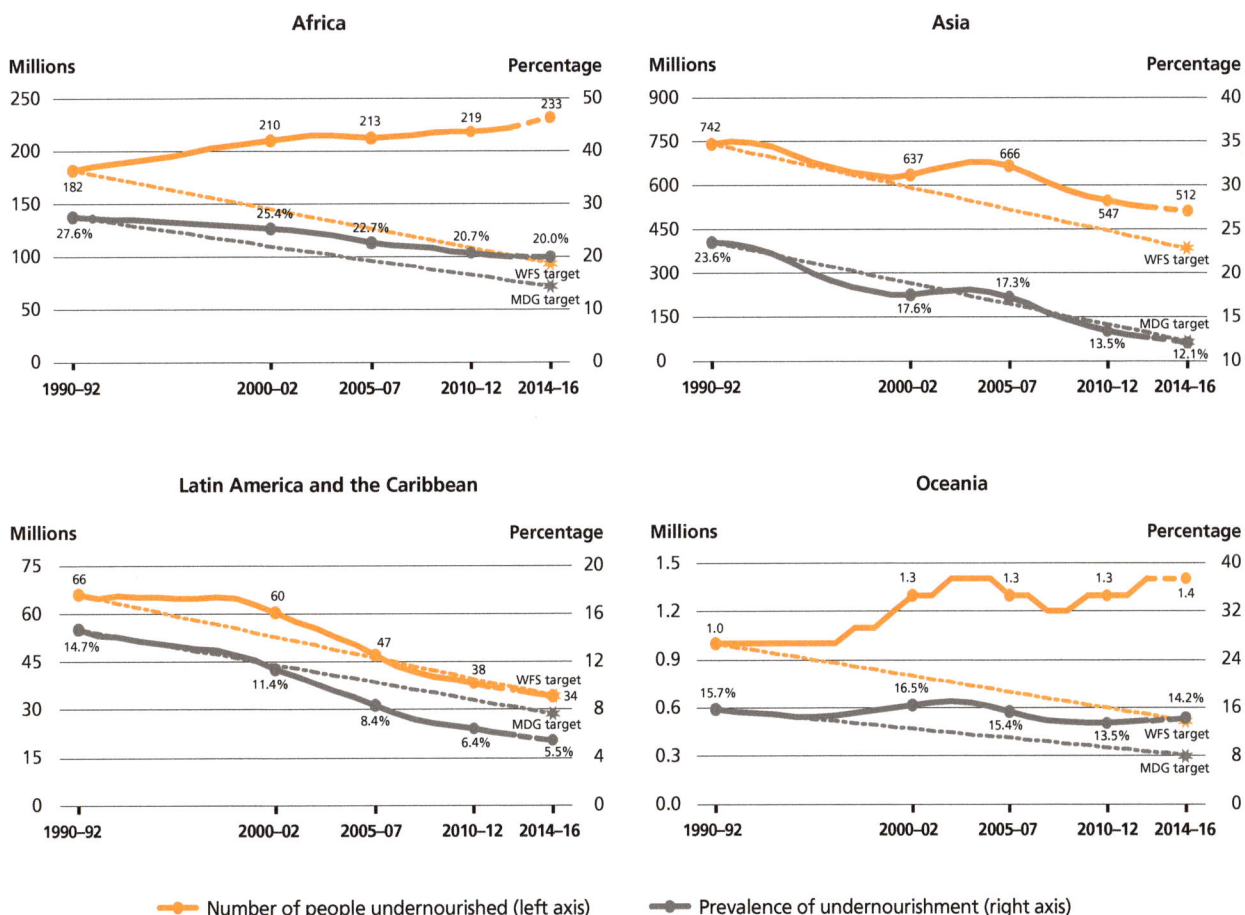

Note: Data for 2014–16 refer to provisional estimates.
Source: FAO.

TABLE **2**

Countries that have achieved, or are close to reaching, the international hunger targets

WFS goal and MDG 1c target achieved	Close to reaching WFS goal*	MDG 1c target achieved	Close to reaching MDG 1c target *	Prevalence of undernourishment below (or close to) 5 percent since 1990
1 Angola	1 Algeria	1 Algeria	1 Cabo Verde	1 Argentina
2 Armenia	2 Indonesia	2 Bangladesh	2 Chad	2 Barbados
3 Azerbaijan	3 Maldives	3 Benin	3 Colombia	3 Brunei Darussalam
4 Brazil	4 Panama	4 Bolivia (Plurinational State of)	4 Ecuador	4 Egypt
5 Cameroon	5 South Africa	5 Cambodia	5 Jamaica	5 Kazakhstan
6 Chile	6 Togo	6 Costa Rica	6 Honduras	6 Lebanon
7 China	7 Trinidad and Tobago	7 Ethiopia	7 Paraguay	7 Republic of Korea
8 Cuba	8 Tunisia	8 Fiji	8 Rwanda	8 Saudi Arabia
9 Djibouti		9 Gambia	9 Sierra Leone	9 South Africa
10 Dominican Republic		10 Indonesia		10 Tunisia
11 Gabon		11 Iran		11 Turkey
12 Georgia		12 Jordan		12 United Arab Emirates
13 Ghana		13 Kiribati		
14 Guyana		14 Lao People's Democratic Republic		
15 Kuwait		15 Malawi		
16 Kyrgyzstan		16 Malaysia		
17 Mali		17 Maldives		
18 Myanmar		18 Mauritania		
19 Nicaragua		19 Mauritius		
20 Oman		20 Mexico		
21 Peru		21 Morocco		
22 Saint Vincent and the Grenadines		22 Mozambique		
23 Samoa		23 Nepal		
24 Sao Tome and Principe		24 Niger		
25 Thailand		25 Nigeria		
26 Turkmenistan		26 Panama		
27 Uruguay		27 Philippines		
28 Venezuela (Bolivarian Republic of)		28 Solomon Islands		
29 Viet Nam		29 Suriname		
		30 Togo		
		31 Uzbekistan		

*These countries are expected to reach the target before the year 2020.
Source: FAO calculations.

Sub-Saharan Africa: some success stories, but the international hunger targets are far from being met

In sub-Saharan Africa, just under one in every four people, or 23.2 percent of the population, is estimated to be undernourished in 2014–16 (Figure 4, p. 14). This is the highest prevalence of undernourishment for any region and, with about 220 million hungry people in 2014–16, the second highest burden in absolute terms. In fact, the number of undernourished people even increased by 44 million between 1990–92 and 2014–16. Taking into account the region's declining PoU (Table 1, p. 8), this reflects the region's remarkably high population growth rate of 2.7 percent per year. The slow pace of progress in fighting hunger over the years is particularly worrisome. While the PoU fell relatively rapidly between 2000–02 and 2005–07, this pace slowed in subsequent years, reflecting factors such as rising food prices, droughts and political instability in several countries.

TABLE **3**

Countries that have achieved the international hunger targets, by region

Sub-Saharan Africa	Eastern, Southern and South-Eastern Asia, and Oceania	Latin America and the Caribbean	Caucasus and Central Asia	Northern Africa and Western Asia
Countries that met the MDG 1c target by halving the proportion of hungry people or bringing it under 5 percent by 2015				
1 Benin	11 Bangladesh	22 Bolivia	27 Uzbekistan	28 Algeria
2 Ethiopia	12 Cambodia	23 Costa Rica		29 Iran
3 Gambia	13 Fiji	24 Mexico		30 Jordan
4 Malawi	14 Indonesia	25 Panama		31 Morocco
5 Mauritania	15 Kiribati	26 Suriname		
6 Mauritius	16 Lao People's Democratic Republic			
7 Mozambique	17 Malaysia			
8 Niger	18 Maldives			
9 Nigeria	19 Nepal			
10 Togo	20 Philippines			
	21 Solomon Islands			
Countries that reached both the MDG 1c target and the WFS goal of halving the number of hungry people by 2015				
1 Angola	8 China	13 Brazil	23 Armenia	28 Kuwait
2 Cameroon	9 Myanmar	14 Chile	24 Azerbaijan	29 Oman
3 Djibouti	10 Samoa	15 Cuba	25 Georgia	
4 Gabon	11 Thailand	16 Dominican Republic	26 Kyrgyzstan	
5 Ghana	12 Viet Nam	17 Guyana	27 Turkmenistan	
6 Mali		18 Nicaragua		
7 Sao Tome and Principe		19 Peru		
		20 Saint Vincent and the Grenadines		
		21 Uruguay		
		22 Venezuela (Bolivarian Republic of)		
Countries that maintained undernourishment below or close to 5 percent since 1990–92				
1 South Africa	2 Brunei Darussalam	4 Argentina	6 Kazakhstan	7 Egypt
	3 Republic of Korea	5 Barbados		8 Turkey
				9 Lebanon
				10 Saudi Arabia
				11 Tunisia
				12 United Arab Emirates

Source: FAO.

In the Central African subregion,[10] the number of undernourished people more than doubled between 1990–92 and 2014–16, while the PoU declined by 23.4 percent. The divergence between the increase in absolute numbers and the decline in the PoU is explained by the Central Africa's rapid population growth. The lack of progress in absolute terms reflects prevailing problems in the subregion, notably political instability, civil strife and outright war, as is the case in the Central African Republic.

Eastern Africa remains the subregion with the biggest hunger problem in absolute terms, being home to 124 million undernourished people. As in Central Africa, the region continues to experience rapid population growth. While the share of undernourished has fallen by 33.2 percent, the number of hungry people has risen by nearly 20 percent over the MDG monitoring period. A more favourable picture emerges in Southern Africa, where the PoU has fallen by 28 percent since 1990–92 and a little more than 3 million people remain undernourished. The most successful subregion in reducing hunger is Western Africa, where the number of undernourished people has decreased by 24.5 percent since

1990–92, while the PoU is projected to be less than 10 percent in 2014–16. This success has been achieved despite a combination of limiting factors, such as rapid population growth – Nigeria is the most populated country in the region – drought in the Sahel and the high food prices experienced in recent years.

A total of 18 countries in sub-Saharan Africa have achieved the MDG 1c hunger target, and four more are close to reaching it (i.e. they are expected to do so before 2020 if current trends persist). Of these, seven countries have also achieved the more ambitious WFS goal (Angola, Cameroon, Djibouti, Gabon, Ghana, Mali and Sao Tome and Principe), and two more (South Africa and Togo) are close to doing so. While these are welcome developments, progress mostly started from high levels of undernourishment, and many of these countries are still burdened with high hunger levels. The more populous countries that have reached the MDG 1c hunger target include Angola, Cameroon, Ethiopia, Ghana, Malawi, Mozambique, Nigeria and Togo. In addition, many smaller countries, including Benin, the Gambia, Mauritius and the Niger have reached MDG 1c. Others, including Chad,

FIGURE 4

Undernourishment trends: progress made in almost all regions, but at very different rates

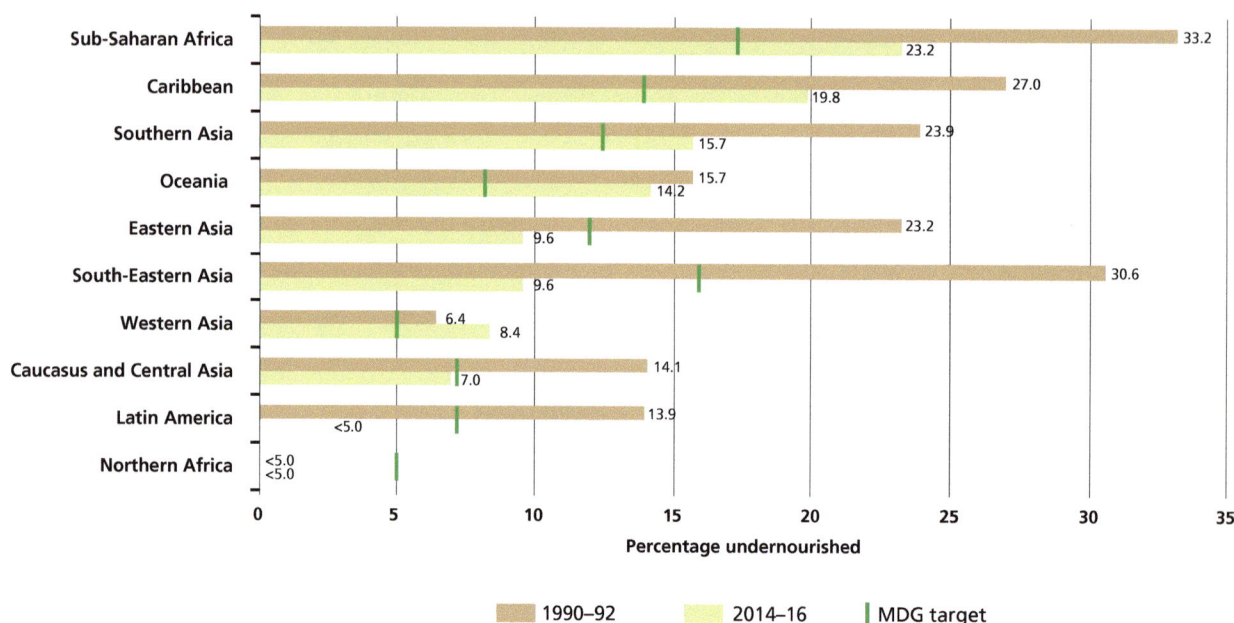

Region	1990–92	2014–16
Sub-Saharan Africa	33.2	23.2
Caribbean	27.0	19.8
Southern Asia	23.9	15.7
Oceania	15.7	14.2
Eastern Asia	23.2	9.6
South-Eastern Asia	30.6	9.6
Western Asia	6.4	8.4
Caucasus and Central Asia	14.1	7.0
Latin America	13.9	<5.0
Northern Africa	<5.0	<5.0

Percentage undernourished

■ 1990–92   ■ 2014–16   ▍ MDG target

Note: Data for 2014–16 refer to provisional estimates.
Source: FAO.

Rwanda and Sierra Leone, are close to reaching the MDG 1c hunger target, even if the hunger burden in these countries remains high, both in relative and absolute terms. However, most countries in sub-Saharan Africa show lack of progress towards the international targets, and many countries, including the Central African Republic and Zambia, still face high PoU levels.

As discussed in more detail in the third section of this report, "Food security and nutrition: the drivers of change" (see pp. 26–42), many of the countries that have made good progress in fighting hunger have enjoyed stable political conditions, overall economic growth and expanding primary sectors, mainly agriculture, fisheries and forestry. Many had policies in place aimed at promoting and protecting access to food. Moreover, many of these countries have experienced high population growth rates, yet have still achieved the MDG 1c target and even the WFS goal.[11] This shows that hunger reduction can be achieved even where populations are increasing rapidly, if adequate policy and institutional conditions are put in place. By contrast, countries where progress has been insufficient or where hunger rates have deteriorated are often characterized by weak agricultural growth and inadequate social protection measures. Many are in a state of protracted crisis. The number of such countries extends beyond those for which data are provided in Table A1. The lack of reliable information on food availability and access prevents a sound analysis of the PoU for countries such as Burundi, the Democratic Republic of the Congo, Eritrea and

Somalia, hence their exclusion, but food security indicators for which data are available suggest that their levels of undernourishment remain very high.

■ **Northern Africa: international hunger targets are met, despite potential instability**

Trends and levels of undernourishment in Northern Africa are very different from those in the rest of the continent. The region has attained PoU levels below 5 percent according to the projections for 2014–16 (Figure 4).[12] The positions of individual countries *vis-à-vis* the international hunger targets are more or less consistent. While 5 percent of the population can still amount to a considerable number of people in Algeria, Egypt, Morocco and Tunisia, the generally low PoU indicates that, based on current trends, the region is close to eradicating severe food insecurity.

Subsidized access to food is a central policy element in the region, with prices for basic foods remaining low in many countries, even when world prices spiked. While the sustainability of these measures can be questioned, they have helped keep levels of undernourishment low, by supplying large amount of calories affordably. The focus on calories, however, has left dietary quality concerns largely unaddressed, giving rise to other forms of malnutrition, including a rising prevalence of overweight and obesity. Moreover, the region remains exposed to potential and actual economic and political instability. Some countries are heavily dependent on

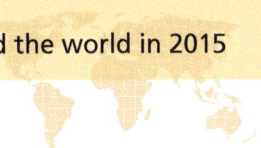

food imports, and their limited resource base, coupled with rapid population growth, suggests that import dependence will remain a feature of the region in the future, notwithstanding efforts to increase agricultural productivity.

Southern Asia: some progress, but too slow to meet the international hunger targets

The highest burden of hunger in absolute terms is to be found in Southern Asia. Estimates for 2014–16 suggest that about 281 million people are undernourished in the region, marking only a slight reduction from the number in 1990–92 (Table 1, p. 8). But there has been noticeable progress in relative terms: the PoU has declined from 23.9 percent in 1990–92 to 15.7 percent in 2014–16 (Figure 4). The region is on a trajectory towards a more manageable hunger burden. Most importantly, progress has accelerated over the last decade, notwithstanding higher prices on international commodity markets. The evolution of hunger trends in India, in particular, has a significant influence on results for the region. Higher world food prices, observed since the late 2000s, have not been entirely transmitted into domestic prices, especially in large countries such as India. In this country, the extended food distribution programme also contributed to this positive outcome. Higher economic growth has not been fully translated into higher food consumption, let alone better diets overall, suggesting that the poor and hungry may have failed to benefit much from overall growth.

Most countries in Southern Asia have made progress towards the international hunger targets, even if the pace has been too slow for them to reach either the WFS or the MDG targets, including, for example, Afghanistan, India, Pakistan and Sri Lanka. As these countries constitute a large share of the region's population, they account for the low overall performance – India still has the second-highest estimated number of undernourished people in the world. A notable exception in terms of performance is Bangladesh, which has made faster progress and has already reached the MDG 1c hunger target, thanks also to the comprehensive National Food Policy framework adopted in the mid-2000s. Nepal, also, has not only reached the MDG 1c hunger target, but has almost reached the 5 percent threshold. One more country in the region, the Islamic Republic of Iran, has already brought the PoU below 5 percent, and has thus reached the MDG 1c target.

Eastern and South-Eastern Asia: rapid and generalized progress towards the international hunger targets

The most successful subregions in fighting hunger have been Eastern and South-Eastern Asia. The number of undernourished people in Eastern Asia has fallen from 295 million in 1990–92 to 145 million in 2014–16, a 50.9 percent reduction (Table 1, p. 8). Over the same period,

the PoU dropped from 23.2 percent at the beginning of the monitoring period, to 9.6 percent in 2014–16, a reduction of more than 60 percent (Figure 4).

In South-Eastern Asia, the number of undernourished people has continued its steady decline, from 137.5 million in 1990–92 to 60.5 million by 2014–16, a 56 percent reduction overall. The PoU has shrunk by a remarkable 68.5 percent, falling from 30.6 percent in 1990–92 to less than 10 percent in 2014–16. Most countries in South-Eastern Asia are making rapid progress towards international targets. Cambodia, Indonesia, the Lao People's Democratic Republic, Malaysia, Myanmar, the Philippines, Thailand and Viet Nam all account for this positive performance. No country in the region shows lack of progress with respect to the international targets. Brunei Darussalam and Malaysia have reduced their PoU to below the 5 percent threshold, which means they are close to having eradicated hunger.

As discussed in more detail in the section "Food security and nutrition: the drivers of change" (pp. 26–42), much of the success of Eastern and South-Eastern Asia was possible due to high overall economic growth. Unlike Southern Asia, these subregions experienced more inclusive growth, with more of the poor and vulnerable sharing the benefits. Rapid productivity growth in agriculture, since the Green Revolution, has boosted food availability and significantly improved access to food for the rural poor.

China's achievements in reducing hunger dominate the overall performance of Eastern Asia. The country accounts for almost two-thirds of the reduction in the number of undernourished people in the developing regions between 1990–92 and 2014–16. China and the Republic of Korea have achieved both the MDG 1c hunger target and the WFS goal. Nevertheless, given the sheer size of its population, China is still home to an estimated 134 million people facing hunger, and the country with the highest number of undernourished people. The prospects of continued growth, the increasing orientation of the economy towards the domestic market, the expansion of economic opportunities in internal areas of the country and the growing ability of the poor to benefit from these developments, have been and will continue to be key factors in hunger reduction. Again, given its size, this also holds at the regional level and has a marked influence on global results. The only major exception to overall favourable progress in the region is the Democratic People's Republic of Korea, which is burdened by continuously high levels of undernourishment and shows little prospect of addressing its problems any time soon.

Caucasus and Central Asia: rapid recovery from the transition to the market economy enabled the international hunger targets to be met

A combination of factors accounts for progress in the Caucasus and Central Asia, including rapid economic growth, a resource-rich environment and remittances. After

a difficult transition in the early 1990s, often characterized by political instability and economic austerity, economic conditions have improved significantly and the political situation has stabilized. This progress has translated into lower hunger burdens throughout the region. Latest estimates point to a steady decline in the PoU, which has contracted from 14.1 percent in 1990–92 to 7.0 percent for 2014–16 (Figure 4, p. 14). The number of undernourished people is much lower than in other Asian subregions – 5.8 million in 2014–16, down from 9.6 million in 1990–92 (Table 1, p. 8).

Progress has been sufficiently rapid to enable both the region as a whole and most countries to achieve the MDG 1c hunger target. Indeed, most countries have attained PoU levels close to, or below, the 5 percent threshold. Armenia, Azerbaijan, Georgia, Kyrgyzstan and Turkmenistan have achieved the WFS goal, while Kazakhstan and Uzbekistan have achieved the MDG 1c hunger target. The only country still lagging behind is Tajikistan,[13] which is making insufficient progress to reach the international targets, and is burdened by a relatively high PoU (33.2 percent in 2014–16).

■ Western Asia: no progress towards the international hunger targets, despite low undernourishment levels in several countries

A less encouraging picture emerges from Western Asia, where very different patterns can be observed. Some countries, including Iraq and Yemen, show high levels of food insecurity and have made slow progress towards improving this situation. Most other countries, on the contrary, have long since attained solid levels of food security, after having brought undernourishment levels below 5 percent. These include politically stable, resource-rich economies, such as Kuwait, Saudi Arabia and the United Arab Emirates, together with Jordan, Lebanon and Oman – all of which have achieved the MDG 1c hunger target; Kuwait and Oman have also achieved the WFS goal. The group also includes rapidly growing and politically stable countries, such as Turkey. In Iraq and Yemen, as well as other countries in the region for which no reliable information is available, political instability, war and civil strife, as well as fragile institutions, are the main factors underlying the lack of progress.[14]

Despite a relatively low number of undernourished people, Western Asia saw an increase in undernourishment throughout the monitoring period: the PoU rose by 32.2 percent between 1990–92 and 2014–16, from 6.4 to 8.4 percent (Figure 4, p. 14). In parallel, rapid population growth has brought about a dramatic increase in the number of undernourished people, from 8 million to nearly 19 million. The region in its entirety, therefore, has not made progress towards reaching either of the international hunger targets, as a result of the polarized situation across countries.

■ Latin America and the Caribbean: international hunger targets have been met, due to rapid progress in South America

In Latin America, the PoU has declined from 13.9 percent in 1990–92 to less than 5 percent in 2014–16 (Figure 4, p. 14). In parallel, the number of undernourished people fell from 58 million to fewer than 27 million (Table 1, p. 8). As in most regions, stark differences can be found across countries and subregions. The Central American subregion, for instance, saw much less progress compared with that of South America and even Latin America overall. While South America has been able to bring undernourishment down by more than 75 percent and eventually to below the 5 percent mark, the PoU for Central America has declined by only 38.2 percent over the MDG monitoring period.

Despite divergent developments within the region, Latin America has achieved both the MDG 1c and WFS targets by large margins. The overall achievements are to a large extent also a reflection of robust progress in its most populous countries. Good overall economic performance, steady output growth in agriculture and successful social protection policies are among the main correlates of progress in the region. The combination of safety nets with special programmes for family farmers and smallholders and targeted support to vulnerable groups, together with broad-based food security interventions such as school-feeding programmes, have contributed significantly to improving food security in the region. At the continental level, important commitments started in 2005 with the Hunger-Free Latin America and the Caribbean Initiative and, through various other initiatives, eventually led to the Plan for Food Security, Nutrition and Hunger Eradication 2025 of the Community of Latin American and Caribbean States (CELAC),[15] adopted by all countries of the region in January 2015 during its third Presidential Summit.

Hunger rates are currently below the 5 percent threshold in Argentina, Brazil, Chile, Costa Rica, Mexico, Uruguay and the Bolivarian Republic of Venezuela, and the WFS hunger goal has been achieved in Argentina, Brazil, Chile, Guyana, Nicaragua, Peru, Uruguay and the Bolivarian Republic of Venezuela. In all, 13 countries in Latin America have achieved the MDG 1c hunger target. Beyond those listed above, these include the Plurinational State of Bolivia, Guyana, Panama, Peru and Suriname. Another four countries, including Colombia, Ecuador, Honduras and Paraguay, are on track to reach the MDG 1c target over the next few years, if current trends persist. Even if some countries, such as Guatemala or El Salvador, appear to be off-track for reaching the international targets, no country in the region has a PoU higher than 20 percent.

The Caribbean as a whole, like Central America, has failed to meet the MDG 1c target. Unlike Central America, however, the remaining hunger burden in almost all Caribbean countries is lower and thus more manageable. The PoU has dropped from 27.0 percent in 1990–92 to 19.8 percent in

2014–16, a 26.6 percent decrease in relative terms. Many individual Caribbean countries, however, have achieved the international targets or are at least close to reaching them. Barbados, Cuba, the Dominican Republic and Saint Vincent and the Grenadines have all attained the MDG 1c hunger target. The latter three have also reached the more demanding WFS goal. Jamaica and Trinidad and Tobago are also very close to reaching the MDG 1c target. The explanation for the region as a whole lagging behind lies in the severe and still largely unabated problems experienced by Haiti – a country hit by recurrent natural disasters, still facing slow growth in food availability *vis-à-vis* population growth and burdened by an increasingly degraded resource base as well as a fragile national economy.[16]

■ Oceania

The developing countries of Oceania have experienced slow progress towards improved food security. The overall PoU in the region fell by less than 10 percent between 1990–92 and 2014–16. This corresponds to an increase in the number of undernourished people of about 0.5 million, or 50 percent. Being largely small island developing states characterized by high dependency on food imports, food security in most countries can be severely affected by external shocks, including international price volatility, adverse weather events and sudden changes in the availability of a few important staples, such as rice. The Pacific Islands face multiple burdens of malnutrition; while hunger has fallen slowly, overweight, obesity and, as a consequence, non-communicable diseases, such as type 2 diabetes and coronary heart disease, are taking a growing toll on the region's health and economic status.

Several countries in the Oceania region covered by this report have achieved the MDG 1c hunger target, including Fiji, Kiribati, Samoa and the Solomon Islands, while Vanuatu has not. Samoa has also reached the more ambitious WFS goal. The situation in Vanuatu has deteriorated dramatically since Cyclone Pam hit the islands in March 2015.[17] Before this catastrophic event, the country had been showing consistent progress in reducing hunger. In the case of Papua New Guinea, by far the most populous country in the region, a detailed assessment has not been possible due to the lack of reliable background data. Overall progress notwithstanding, there is considerable uncertainty about the situation in the country, where the information needed to reliably estimate undernourishment is largely absent. Anecdotal evidence indicates that the country's food security situation is far from resolved.

Key findings

- **Based on the latest estimates, about 795 million people remain undernourished globally, down 167 million over the last decade, and 216 million lower than in 1990–92. This means that just over one in every nine people in the world are currently unable to consume enough food to conduct an active and healthy life.**

- **About 780 million people, or the vast majority of the hungry, live in the developing regions. In these regions, the prevalence of undernourishment has dropped by 44.4 percent since 1990–92, and the overall share now stands at 12.9 percent of the total population.**

- **The year 2015 marks the end of the monitoring period for the World Food Summit (WFS) and Millennium Development Goal (MDG) hunger targets. The latest projections suggest that, as a whole, the developing regions have almost reached the MDG 1c hunger target. From a statistical perspective, the target was missed by a small margin, but from a development perspective,** the essence of the MDG 1c commitment has been fulfilled, at least globally. The WFS target, by contrast, has been missed by a large margin. The estimated number of undernourished people is some 285 million above the envisaged target for 2015.

- **Wide differences persist across regions. Some have made rapid progress in reducing hunger: Latin America as well as the Eastern and South-Eastern regions of Asia have all achieved both the MDG 1c hunger target and the more ambitious WFS goal. The MDG 1c target has been reached in the Caucasus and Central Asia and in the Northern and Western regions of Africa. Progress has also been recorded in the Caribbean, Oceania, Southern Asia, and Southern and Eastern Africa, but at too slow a pace to reach the MDG 1c target. Finally, Central Africa and Western Asia are moving away from the hunger targets, with a higher proportion of undernourished in the population now than in 1990–92.**

- A total of 72 developing countries of the 129 monitored have reached the MDG 1c hunger target. Of these, 29 countries have also achieved the more ambitious WFS goal. Another 12 countries, among the 72 countries considered to have achieved the MDG 1c target, have maintained the prevalence of undernourishment below, or very close to, 5 percent since 1990–92.

- Most countries that have achieved the international hunger targets enjoyed stable political conditions and economic growth, accompanied by sound social protection policies targeted towards vulnerable population groups. In these countries, the commitment to fight food insecurity proved successful in spite of the difficulties posed by rapid population growth, volatile commodity prices, high food and energy prices, rising unemployment and the economic recessions that occurred in the late 1990s and again after 2008.

- In several countries that have failed to reach the international hunger targets, natural and human-induced disasters or political instability have generated a status of protracted crisis, which has prevented the protection of vulnerable population groups and the promotion of income opportunities for all. In other countries, the benefits of economic growth have failed to reach the poor population, due to lack of effective social protection and income redistribution policies. In the short run, the only means to address food insecurity is humanitarian intervention. In the medium and the long term, hunger eradication can only be pursued if all stakeholders contribute to designing and enacting policies for improving economic opportunities, the protection of vulnerable groups and disaster preparedness. Action undertaken at the global and regional levels should take into account country specificities and exposure to natural and human-induced disasters, especially those of small island developing states.

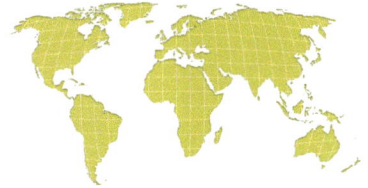

Inside the hunger target: comparing trends in undernourishment and underweight in children

Progress towards the MDG "hunger target", or MDG target 1c, which requires halving, between 1990 and 2015, the proportion of people who suffer from hunger, is measured by two different indicators: the prevalence of undernourishment (PoU), monitored by FAO, and the prevalence of underweight children under five years of age (CU5), monitored by the United Nations Children's Fund (UNICEF) and the World Health Organization (WHO). The end of the MDG monitoring period offers a good opportunity to look back at the evolution of these indicators and to identify common trends, but also to understand the reasons for possible deviations.

Common trends should be discernible as both indicators were approved by the international community to measure the hunger target. Deviations, however, could arise from the different methods used to compile them[18] and the different dimensions of food insecurity that they are expected to capture.

Understanding the different trends of the two indicators across regions and over time is important, as it may offer insights into the complexity of food security, and possibly lead to more targeted policy interventions. Underweight can be caused by a range of different factors – not only calorie or protein deficiency, but also poor hygiene, disease or limited access to clean water. All these factors impede the body's ability to absorb nutrients from food and eventually result in manifestations of nutrient deficits such as stunting, wasting or underweight. For this reason, the two indicators do not always reflect the same underlying problem. Where lack of sufficient food is the main cause of underweight, the PoU and the CU5 should move synchronously. Where poor food utilization prevails instead, the two indicators are likely to diverge.

Considering the developing regions as a whole for the entire MDG monitoring period, the two indicators show consistent trends. From 1990 to 2013, the CU5 moved from 27.4 percent to 16.6 percent, a 39.3 percent reduction, while the PoU declined by 44.5 percent between 1990–92 and 2014–16 (Table 4, Figure 5, pp. 20–21).[19] The annual rate of decline is similar.

Regional patterns

The parallel progress of the two indicators for the developing regions as a whole is not always evident when the analysis focuses on individual regions. In some, the PoU and CU5 indicators show different rates of reduction (Table 4). Within sub-Saharan Africa, for instance, the PoU and the CU5 only move together for Eastern Africa, while they diverge over time for almost all other subregions. By contrast, trends in the subregions in Asia and in Latin America and the Caribbean largely move in parallel. The rest of this section will analyse these divergences and similarities in trends.

■ Northern Africa

The region's problems are well captured by MDG hunger indicators. Both the PoU and CU5 show low absolute levels of food insecurity, even more so than for other developing regions. In particular, the CU5 declined rapidly over the monitoring period, with a reduction from 9.5 to 4.8 percent. Food utilization conditions appear favourable in the region, with more than 90 percent of the population having access to clean water and improved sanitation

TABLE **4**

Prevalence of undernourishment and prevalence of underweight in children under five years of age: progress during the MDG monitoring period

	Prevalence of undernourishment[1]			Prevalence of child underweight[2]		
	Initial	Final	Average annual change	Initial	Final	Average annual change
			(%)			(%)
DEVELOPING REGIONS	**23.3**	**12.9**	**−2.4**	**27.4**	**16.6**	**−2.1**
Africa	**27.6**	**20.00**	**−1.3**	**22.8**	**17.0**	**−1.3**
Northern Africa	<5	<5	−2.9	9.5	4.8	−2.9
Sub-Saharan Africa	33.2	23.2	−1.5	28.5	21.1	−1.3
Eastern Africa	47.2	31.5	−1.7	26.9	18.7	−1.6
Middle Africa	33.5	41.3	0.9	25.0	15.5	−2.1
Southern Africa	7.2	5.2	−1.4	11.9	12.1	0.1
Western Africa	24.2	9.6	−3.8	26.1	20.5	−1.0
Asia	**23.6**	**12.1**	**−2.8**	**31.4**	**18.4**	**−2.3**
Caucasus and Central Asia	14.1	7.0	−2.9	9.3*	4.3	−3.3
Eastern Asia	23.2	9.6	−3.6	14.1	2.7	−6.9
Southern Asia	23.9	15.7	−1.7	49.2	30.0	−2.1
South-Eastern Asia	30.6	9.6	−4.7	30.4	16.6	−2.6
Western Asia	6.4	8.4	1.3	13.0	5.4	−3.8
Latin America and the Caribbean	**14.7**	**5.5**	**−4.0**	**7.0**	**2.7**	**−4.1**
Caribbean	27.0	19.8	−1.3	8.1	3.2	−3.9
Central America	10.7	6.6	−2.0	10.6	3.6	−4.6
Southern America	15.1	<5	−5.7	5.9	2.9	−3.1
Oceania	**15.7**	**14.2**	**−0.4**	**18.5**	**18.9**	**0.1**

Notes:
[1]The initial and final monitoring periods for the prevalence of undernourishment are 1990–92 and 2014–16, respectively.
[2]The initial and final periods for the prevalence of child underweight are 1991 and 2013, respectively. The 1991 estimates are the result of the linear trend between the 1990 and the 1995 official UNICEF estimates (source: http://data.unicef.org/resources/2013/webapps/nutrition#).
*The initial monitoring period for Caucasus and Central Asia was 1995.
Source: FAO and UNICEF/WHO/World Bank.

facilities in 2012. The PoU has remained below the 5 percent threshold since 1990–92 (Figure 6). Many countries of the region have not only sufficient, but excessive levels of calorie availability. Just as in Western Africa, much of the problem lies in unbalanced diets with too many calories from carbohydrates, which are mostly derived from cereals and sugar. Food consumption subsidies, which are granted in several Northern African countries, have played a part in maintaining undernourishment at low levels, while at the same time favouring an excessive consumption of energy-intense foods, potentially leading to increased risks of non-communicable diseases and obesity.

■ **Sub-Saharan Africa**

For the region as a whole, undernourishment and child underweight were looming large at the beginning of the 1990s, with both indicators exceeding 25 percent. Since then, the PoU and CU5 have decreased at a similarly slow pace (Figure 7).

During the 1990s, per capita GDP decreased in a number of sub-Saharan countries, and the region's Human Development Index was the lowest in the world.[20] These factors explain the slow decline in undernourishment, as well as the sluggish investment in infrastructure and health.[21] On average, during the 1990s, only one in four

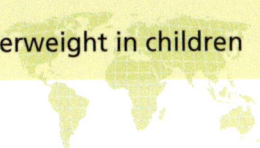

FIGURE **5**

Developing regions: trends in the prevalence of undernourishment and child underweight

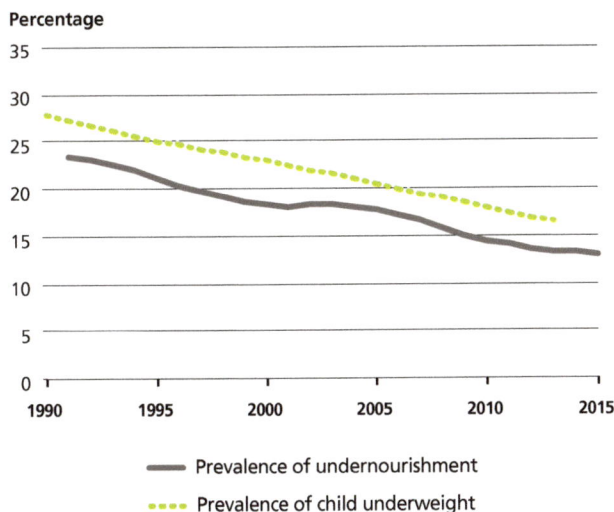

Percentage

— Prevalence of undernourishment

···· Prevalence of child underweight

Note: The prevalence of undernourishment is estimated as a three-year average centred on the years shown on the x-axis. Hence, for example, "2015" corresponds to the estimate for 2014–16.
Sources: FAO and UNICEF/WHO/World Bank.

FIGURE **6**

Northern Africa: trends in the prevalence of undernourishment and child underweight

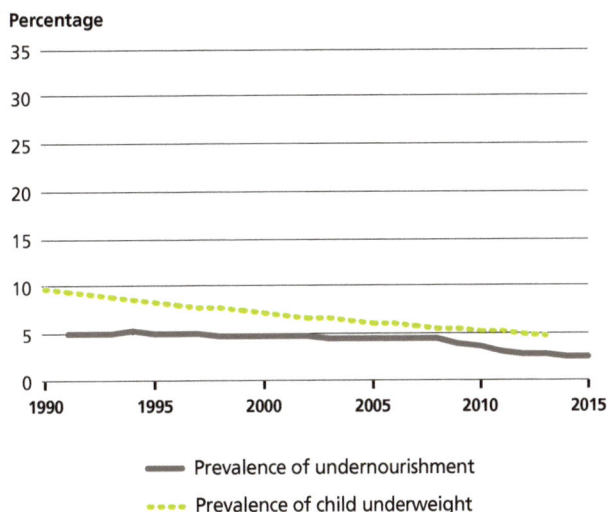

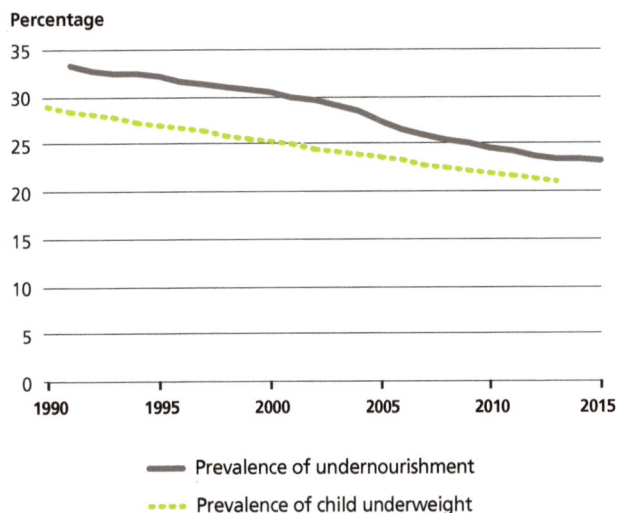

Percentage

— Prevalence of undernourishment

···· Prevalence of child underweight

Note: The prevalence of undernourishment is estimated as a three-year average centred on the years shown on the x-axis. Hence, for example, "2015" corresponds to the estimate for 2014–16.
Sources: FAO and UNICEF/WHO/World Bank.

people had access to electricity, compared with a world average of one in three. Likewise, there were only 0.15 physicians available for every thousand people, compared with a world average of 1.3.

Over the 2000s, the food security situation in sub-Saharan Africa gradually improved. Economic growth resumed in several countries, resulting in a decline of the PoU, but major challenges remained unaddressed, especially in terms of addressing the region's inadequate hygiene conditions and quality of diets. This divergence appears particularly evident for Western Africa. Here, the PoU has fallen by over 60 percent since 1990–92, owing to the progress of large countries such as Ghana and Nigeria. These changes, however, were largely brought about by the higher availability of staple foods, which did not address the dietary imbalances in the region. While the PoU for Western Africa fell rapidly, the CU5 remained stubbornly high, at levels of more than 20 percent.

Sub-Saharan Africa's problems not only illustrate the multifaceted nature of food security, but also suggest that different dimensions require different approaches to successfully improve food security. For instance, making even more carbohydrates available is unlikely to further improve overall food security. Rather, new measures should focus on the ability of poor people to access balanced diets and on overall living conditions, to prevent negative health outcomes such as underweight, wasting and stunting in children.

FIGURE **7**

Sub-Saharan Africa: trends in the prevalence of undernourishment and child underweight

Percentage

— Prevalence of undernourishment

···· Prevalence of child underweight

Note: The prevalence of undernourishment is estimated as a three-year average centred on the years shown on the x-axis. Hence, for example, "2015" corresponds to the estimate for 2014–16.
Sources: FAO and UNICEF/WHO/World Bank.

■ Caucasus and Central Asia

The region has had overall low rates and has made good progress over time for both the PoU and CU5 indicators (Figure 8). The economic and political transitions of the early 1990s and, later, the economic crisis of the early 2000s only seem to have influenced the PoU, which exhibited marked swings during these periods. The two indicators were again moving in parallel by the early 2000s, with improvements in living conditions. In recent years, the CU5 has maintained levels below 5 percent in most countries, with the exception of Tajikistan, where it remains at about 15 percent. Since the early 1990s, only few countries have occasionally presented CU5 values above 10 percent. At the same time, the transition turmoil barely affected the region's overall health and hygiene conditions. The proportion of the population with access to clean water and improved sanitation facilities has always been higher than 85 percent and 90 percent, respectively, throughout the monitoring period. These conditions, together with the improvement in nutrition experienced during the past decade, explain the steady downward trend in the CU5. It is worth highlighting that the high poverty rates experienced by most countries were limited to relatively short periods of time and did not significantly worsen food utilization.

■ Eastern Asia

Steady and rapid progress for both indicators is observed in Eastern Asia. At the beginning of the monitoring period, the PoU declined slightly faster than the CU5 (Figure 9).

The region's average PoU saw some minor ups and downs in the 1990s and the early 2000s, while the reduction in undernourishment accelerated again after 2006.

The more consistent decline in the CU5 can be traced to the steady improvement of hygiene conditions in several countries. Access to safe water, for example, increased by 37 percent over the monitoring period, while access to improved sanitation facilities has increased by 153 percent since the early 1990s. These factors have had a strong positive impact on food utilization, and support both the low CU5 levels and its rapid improvement over time.

■ Southern Asia

Southern Asia is the region with the highest historical CU5 levels, but is also the region where rapid progress has been made in reducing underweight among young children. The prevalence of underweight children declined from 49.2 percent in 1990 to 30.0 percent in 2013, with a 39.0 percent reduction over the MDG monitoring period (Table 4, p. 20). By contrast, the PoU in Southern Asia made less progress overall, resulting in a convergence between the two indicators over time (Figure 10).

There is growing evidence that helps explain the relatively rapid decline of the CU5. Many countries in the region have experienced robust economic growth over the past 25 years, bringing down poverty rates. While the steady decline in child underweight is consistent with the decrease in poverty, undernourishment only went down

FIGURE **8**

Causasus and Central Asia: trends in the prevalence of undernourishment and child underweight

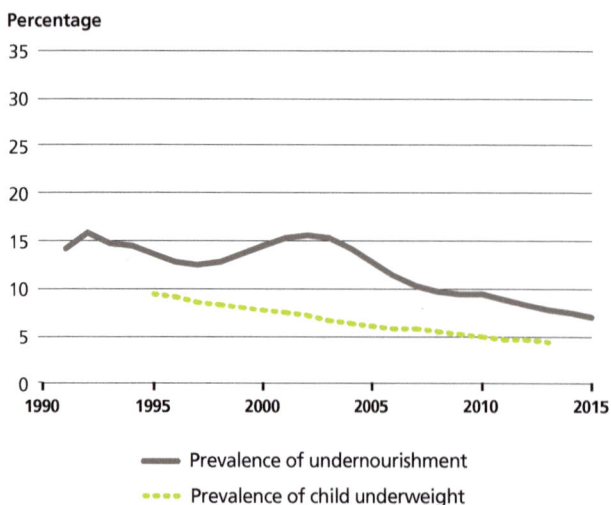

Percentage

Note: The prevalence of undernourishment is estimated as a three-year average centred on the years shown on the x-axis. Hence, for example, "2015" corresponds to the estimate for 2014–16.
Sources: FAO and UNICEF/WHO/World Bank.

FIGURE **9**

Eastern Asia: trends in the prevalence of undernourishment and child underweight

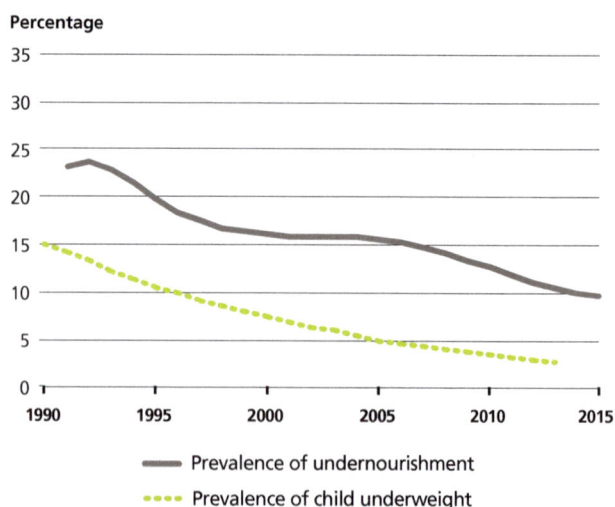

Percentage

Note: The prevalence of undernourishment is estimated as a three-year average centred on the years shown on the x-axis. Hence, for example, "2015" corresponds to the estimate for 2014–16.
Sources: FAO and UNICEF/WHO/World Bank.

FIGURE **10**

Southern Asia: trends in the prevalence of undernourishment and child underweight

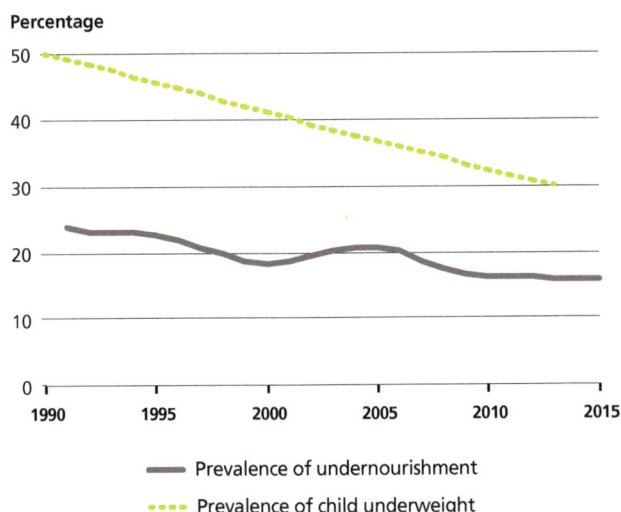

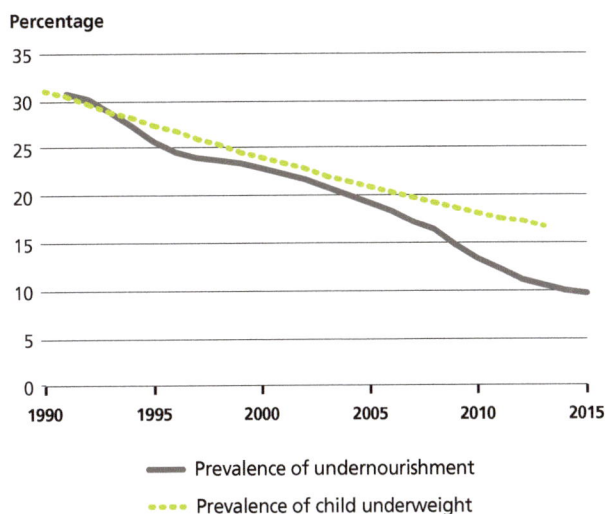

Percentage

- Prevalence of undernourishment
- - - - Prevalence of child underweight

Note: The prevalence of undernourishment is estimated as a three-year average centred on the years shown on the x-axis. Hence, for example, "2015" corresponds to the estimate for 2014–16.
Sources: FAO and UNICEF/WHO/World Bank.

FIGURE **11**

South-Eastern Asia: trends in the prevalence of undernourishment and child underweight

Percentage

- Prevalence of undernourishment
- - - - Prevalence of child underweight

Note: The prevalence of undernourishment is estimated as a three-year average centred on the years shown on the x-axis. Hence, for example, "2015" corresponds to the estimate for 2014–16.
Sources: FAO and UNICEF/WHO/World Bank.

from 23.9 percent to 15.7 percent between 1990–92 and 2014–16. This different pattern is largely due to India, the country that more directly affects the regional picture as a result of its large population. Explanations offered for the inconsistency between food consumption and income levels in India range from increasing inequalities, to poor data, to the challenges of capturing the changing energy requirements of the population.[22] But the puzzle still seems to be unresolved; and, as noted in the previous section, calorie consumption is lower than what per capita incomes and poverty rates would suggest.

The reasons for CU5 progress include enhanced access to safe water and sanitation and, as a consequence, better hygiene and health conditions. For instance, household access to improved sanitation nearly doubled from 23 percent to 42 percent between 1990 and 2012. Over the same period, access to safe water rose from 73 percent to 91 percent. In addition, targeted nutrition programmes in key countries in the region, aimed at young children, pregnant women and women of reproductive age, likely contributed to a rapidly declining CU5. Examples include, among others, the Integrated Child Development Scheme, implemented in India since 1975, and the Bangladesh Integrated Nutrition Programme, funded by the World Bank. Despite the rapid decrease in the CU5, the indicator was still much higher compared with those of all other Asian subregions. This suggests that much more progress can be achieved in the future by combining policy interventions that enhance both food availability and utilization.

■ **South-Eastern Asia**

South-Eastern Asia is among the regions that showed faster progress across the first seven MDGs. This also holds for the hunger target as measured by both the PoU and CU5. Undernourishment and underweight in children were both above 30 percent at the beginning of the monitoring period (Figure 11), but the PoU declined more quickly throughout the 2000s. This would be in line with the view that policy interventions to improve hygiene conditions – for instance water and sanitation infrastructure – typically require higher investments compared with those aimed at enhancing food availability. The CU5 has declined rapidly in the region, but is still above 20 percent in more than one country. Rapid progress has been made in improving hygiene conditions, with 71 percent of the population having access to better sanitation.[23] In view of the good growth prospects in the region, this also means that more progress will be possible, provided that interventions improve the diets of poor population groups and ensure wider access to clean water and sanitation facilities.

■ **Western Asia**

Western Asia shows a unique pattern of change. While the PoU has increased since the early 1990s, reflecting political instability in a number of countries, the CU5 has continued to decline. Underweight in children is at a low level virtually everywhere, while the sparse data available indicate high

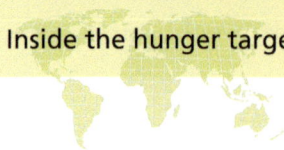

proportions in Yemen – well beyond 20 percent – and to a lower extent in other countries, such as Iraq and Syria, where data for the 2000s point to shares not far from 10 percent. Hygiene conditions in the region are generally good, with more than 90 percent of the population having access to clean water sources, and 88 percent of the population having access to improved sanitation facilities in 2012. The rise in the PoU, as shown in the previous section, reflects political and social problems together with war and civil strife in a limited number of countries in the region, which generated large migrant and refugee populations (Figure 12).

■ Latin America and the Caribbean

In the region as a whole, the two hunger indicators have converged over time, at a faster rate after the year 2000, when progress in reducing the PoU accelerated. The PoU, estimated at 14.7 percent in 1990–92, dropped to 5.5 percent by 2014–16, while the CU5 has decreased from 7.0 percent to 2.7 percent over the same period (Figure 13). The CU5 is generally low, with few exceptions. Within the region, Central America remains the most problematic area, with almost no improvement recorded over the MDG monitoring period. The PoU and the CU5 in Central America were close to each other in the early 1990s (at about 11 percent of the population) and both indicators have seen little progress since then. Shares higher than 10 percent have been reported for Haiti in recent periods; in this country the

indicator has decreased since the early 1990s, when it exceeded 20 percent. Relatively high values have been reported, in recent years, also for Guatemala, Honduras and Guyana, although not exceeding 15 percent.

Progress for both indicators stems from economic growth combined with a stronger commitment to social protection, especially over the last decade. Many countries have made hunger and malnutrition eradication a high political priority. At the continental level, important commitments started in 2005 with the Hunger-Free Latin America and the Caribbean Initiative, and eventually led, through various other initiatives, to the *Santiago Declaration of the Community of Latin American and Caribbean States* in January 2013. Despite progress, major challenges remain. Many countries are witnessing growing overweight and obesity rates and, as a result, the increasing prevalence of non-communicable diseases.

■ Oceania

This region is characterized by high rates of underweight among children. Without progress over 25 years, the CU5 is now not far from levels prevalent in many parts of sub-Saharan Africa. Slow progress is also observed for the PoU (Figure 14). The common trends for the two indicators suggest related underlying drivers, especially low food availability and dietary diversity. In many small island developing states in the region, the variety of nutrients available and acquired is somewhat limited.

FIGURE **12**

Western Asia: trends in the prevalence of undernourishment and child underweight

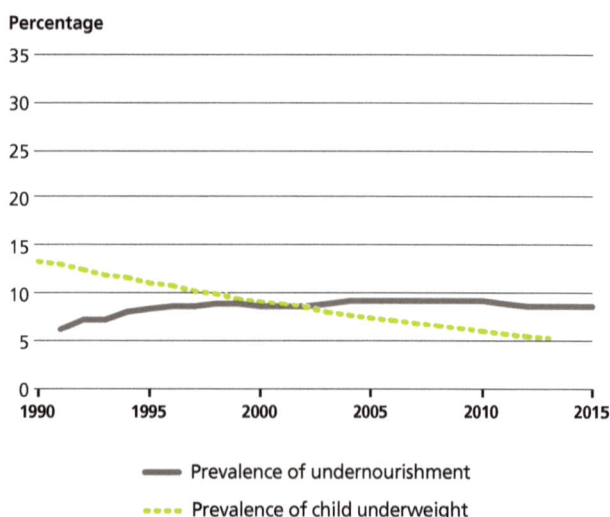

Percentage

Prevalence of undernourishment
Prevalence of child underweight

Note: The prevalence of undernourishment is estimated as a three-year average centred on the years shown on the x-axis. Hence, for example, "2015" corresponds to the estimate for 2014–16.
Sources: FAO and UNICEF/WHO/World Bank.

FIGURE **13**

Latin America and the Caribbean: trends in the prevalence of undernourishment and child underweight

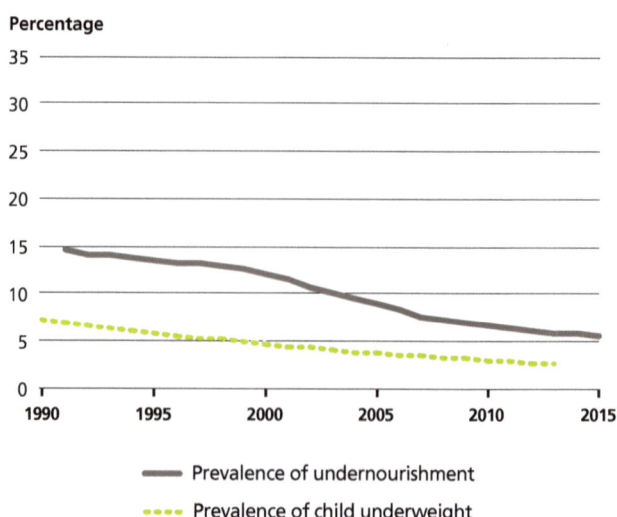

Percentage

Prevalence of undernourishment
Prevalence of child underweight

Note: The prevalence of undernourishment is estimated as a three-year average centred on the years shown on the x-axis. Hence, for example, "2015" corresponds to the estimate for 2014–16.
Sources: FAO and UNICEF/WHO/World Bank.

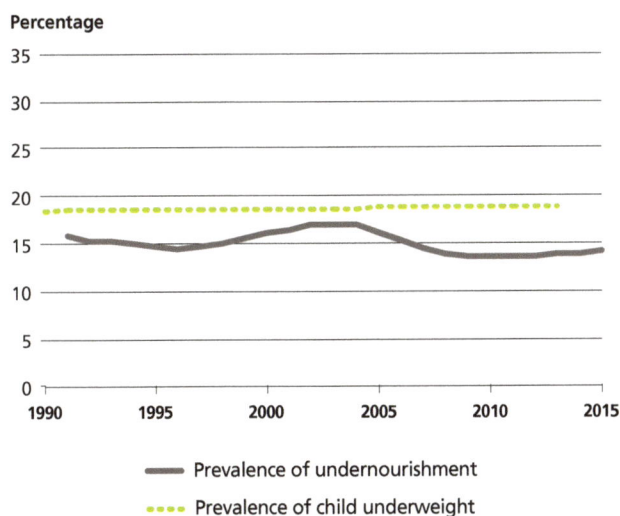

FIGURE **14**

Oceania: trends in the prevalence of undernourishment and child underweight

Percentage

Note: The prevalence of undernourishment is estimated as a three-year average centred on the years shown on the x-axis. Hence, for example, "2015" corresponds to the estimate for 2014–16.
Sources: FAO and UNICEF/WHO/World Bank.

Slow progress in increasing access to safe drinking water and improved sanitation facilities has also contributed to lack of progress in reducing food insecurity. Only 55 percent of households in the region have access to safe water, while only 35 percent have access to improved sanitation facilities. Several indicators for the underlying drivers even suggest some deterioration of the situation. While access to safe water has improved by just 12 percent since the early 1990s, access to sanitation facilities has declined by about 1 percent per year over the same period.

Moreover, the region suffers from a malnutrition problem not well captured by the PoU and CU5, namely the growing coexistence of undernutrition and overnutrition. One contributing factor to overnutrition has been the "westernization" of food consumption patterns, which is associated with a rising prevalence of overweight and obesity.

Key findings

- For the world as a whole, the MDG 1 indicators for prevalence of undernourishment and underweight children under 5 years of age have largely moved in parallel, providing a consistent message regarding achievement of the hunger target. At the regional level, however, noticeable divergences have emerged and often persisted. These differences can often be traced back to different rates of progress in improving the quality of diets and in improving hygiene conditions and access to clean water. These factors affect people's ability to derive sound nutrition from the food they consume.

- Underweight in children is expected to decline less rapidly than undernourishment, given that better hygiene conditions, access to clean water and more varied diets usually require more investment and more time to materialize than enhanced availability of calories. This has been the case in South-Eastern Asia, where undernourishment has declined at a faster rate than child underweight, especially throughout the 2000s, indicating that there is still room for improving dietary quality, particularly for poorer population groups. A similar situation is found in Northern Africa, where carbohydrate-rich diets keeps undernourishment under control, but a lack of dietary quality and diversity has pushed child malnutrition to relatively high levels.

- Despite showing rapid reduction, Southern Asia is the region with the highest historical prevalence of underweight children among the developing regions. Factors such as poor health and inadequate hygiene conditions have held back progress towards improving overall food security. These factors may deserve more attention in future efforts to improve food security at the country level.

- In sub-Saharan Africa, there has been limited progress in reducing both undernourishment and child underweight. This suggests that all aspects of food security need to be tackled – including ensuring the availability of, and access to, more and better quality food, enhanced hygiene conditions and access to clean water – before significant progress towards improved food security can be made.

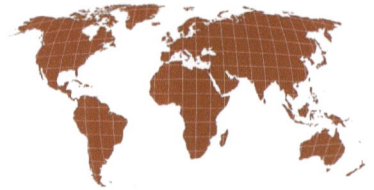

Food security and nutrition: the drivers of change

In 2000, world leaders met and adopted the United Nations Millennium Declaration. Later, eight Millennium Development Goals (MDGs) were set out, including the first one on halving hunger and extreme poverty rates, reflecting the world's commitment to improving the lives of billions of people.

Half a year remains before the end of 2015, the deadline for achieving most of the MDG targets, including the hunger target, MDG 1c, traditionally measured using the prevalence of undernourishment (PoU) indicator. As this report shows, since 1990–92, over 216 million people have been rescued from a life of hunger – to date, 72 countries have already reached the MDG 1c hunger target, with another nine just short by a small margin. Of these, 12 developing countries already had undernourishment rates below 5 percent in 1990–92. Meanwhile, twenty-nine countries have accomplished the more ambitious 1996 World Food Summit (WFS) goal of halving the number of chronically underfed people (Tables 2 and 3, pp. 12–13).

Progress towards food security and nutrition targets requires that food is available, accessible and of sufficient quantity and quality to ensure good nutritional outcomes. Proper nutrition contributes to human development; it helps people realize their full potential and take advantage of opportunities offered by the development process. As past editions of this report (2010, 2012 and 2014) have shown, good governance, political stability and the rule of law, and the absence of conflict and civil strife, weather-related shocks or excessive food price volatility, are conducive to all dimensions of food security.

This section looks at a range of factors that enable progress towards food security and nutrition goals. The list of factors – economic growth, agricultural productivity growth, markets (including international trade) and social protection – is by no means exhaustive. The section also shows how being in a protracted crisis has deleterious effects on progress in hunger reduction. Preliminary quantitative analysis, using data from the period 1992–2013, has helped identify these drivers of change and their relative importance in shaping progress against hunger.[24]

Economic growth is central to the fight against hunger – countries that become richer are less susceptible to food insecurity. Policy-makers in rapidly growing economies have increased capacity and resources to dedicate to improving food security and nutrition. But this is not always the case. Economic growth, while a necessary condition for progress in poverty and hunger reduction, especially in the face of an expanding population, is not sufficient. It is *inclusive* growth that matters – growth that promotes equitable access to food, assets and resources, particularly for poor people and women, so that individuals can develop their potential.[25]

Across the developing world, the majority of the poor and most of the hungry live in rural areas, where family farming and smallholder agriculture is a prevailing – albeit not universal – mode of farm organization. Although the ability of family farming and smallholder agriculture to spur growth through productivity increases varies considerably, its role in reducing poverty and hunger is key. Growth in family farming and smallholder agriculture, through labour and land productivity increases, has significant positive effects on the livelihoods of the poor through increases in food availability and incomes.

The linkages between food security and international trade are complex and context-specific. Policies that affect exports and imports of food contribute to determining relative prices, wages and incomes in the domestic market, and hence shape the ability of poor people to access food. Trade, in itself, is neither a threat nor a panacea when it comes to food security. The opportunities and risks to food security associated with trade openness should be carefully assessed and addressed through an expanded set of policy instruments.

Social protection systems have become an important tool in the fight against hunger. More than one hundred countries implement conditional or unconditional cash transfer programmes that focus on promoting food security and nutrition, health and education, particularly for children. Food distribution schemes and employment guarantee programmes are also important. The expansion of social protection across the developing world has been critical for progress towards the MDG 1c hunger target. Providing regular and predictable cash transfers to poor households often plays a critical role in terms of filling immediate food gaps, but can also help improve the lives and livelihoods of the poor by alleviating constraints to their productive capacity. Combining social protection with complementary agricultural development

measures, such as the Purchase from Africans for Africa programme, which links family farmers and smallholders to school-feeding programmes, can maximize the poverty-reducing impact of these programmes.

In 1990, only 12 countries in Africa were facing food crises, of which only four were in protracted crises.[26] Just 20 years later, a total of 24 countries were experiencing food crises, with 19 in crisis for eight or more of the previous ten years. Food insecurity can be both a cause and effect of protracted crises and can be instrumental in triggering or deepening conflict and civil strife – it increasingly lies at the root of protracted crisis situations. The impact of conflict on food security can be more dramatic than the direct impact of war, and mortality caused by conflict through food insecurity, and famine can far exceed deaths directly caused by violence.[27]

Economic growth and progress towards food security and nutrition targets

Economic growth is necessary for alleviating poverty and reducing hunger and malnutrition; it is critical for sustainably increasing employment and incomes, especially in low-income countries. Since the beginning of the 1990s and up to 2013 (most of the MDG monitoring period) global output per capita has increased by 1.3 percent per year, on average. The economies of low- and middle-income countries – including all developing countries – grew more rapidly, by 3.4 percent per year. Nevertheless, these numbers mask considerable variation in economic growth performance across regions and countries.

The relationship between economic growth and hunger is complex. Economic growth increases household incomes, through higher wages, increased employment opportunities, or both, due to stronger demand for labour. In a growing economy, more household members are able to find work and earn incomes. This is essential for improving food security and nutrition and contributes to a virtuous circle as better nutrition strengthens human capacities and productivity, thus leading to better economic performance. However, the question here is whether or not those people who are living in extreme poverty and are most affected by hunger will be given the opportunity to participate in the benefits of growth and, if they are, whether they will be able to take advantage of it.

On average, and across the developing world since 1990–92, economic growth has brought strong and persistent hunger reduction. This is evident when GDP per capita is plotted against the PoU (Figure 15, p. 28). Increases in the incomes of the poor are associated with higher intake of dietary energy and other nutrients. But in the longer term, as economies grow and countries become richer, this relationship weakens – increases in GDP may bring relatively fewer people out of hunger (in Figure 15, the line reflecting the relationship between economic growth and the PoU was steeper in 1992 than in 2010). Among the early success stories is Ghana, which has experienced average annual growth rates of over 3 percent, and has witnessed impressive hunger reduction rates – the PoU in the country fell from 47 percent in 1990–92 to below 5 percent in 2012–14 (Box 1, p. 29).

In several cases, the positive effects of economic growth on food security and nutrition are related to greater participation of women in the labour force. In Brazil, for example, labour force participation of women rose from 45 percent in 1990–94 to 60 percent in 2013. In Costa Rica, the proportion of women workers increased by 23 percent between 2000 and 2008. Spending by women typically involves more household investments in food and nutrition, but also in health, sanitation and education, compared with the case when resources are controlled by men.[28]

But not all countries that experienced strong economic growth performed well in terms of hunger reduction. Some countries progressed well towards the international hunger targets, while others experienced setbacks. In general, there has been uneven progress in translating economic growth into improvements in food security.

■ Inclusive economic growth and poverty reduction

On the whole, progress in alleviating poverty has been faster than in fighting hunger. This is because the hungry are the poorest of the poor; they have limited or no access to physical and financial assets, little or no education, and often suffer from ill health. Poor agricultural households lack access to sufficient, high-quality land and other natural resources or to remunerative sources of income (self-employment, wage labour). At the same time, hunger creates a trap from which people cannot easily escape. Hunger and undernutrition mean less-productive individuals, who are more prone to disease and thus often unable to earn more and improve their livelihoods. This, in turn, hinders progress in alleviating extreme poverty and fighting hunger – particularly as labour is the principal asset held by the poor.

FIGURE **15**

Economic growth and prevalence of undernourishment, 1992, 2000 and 2010

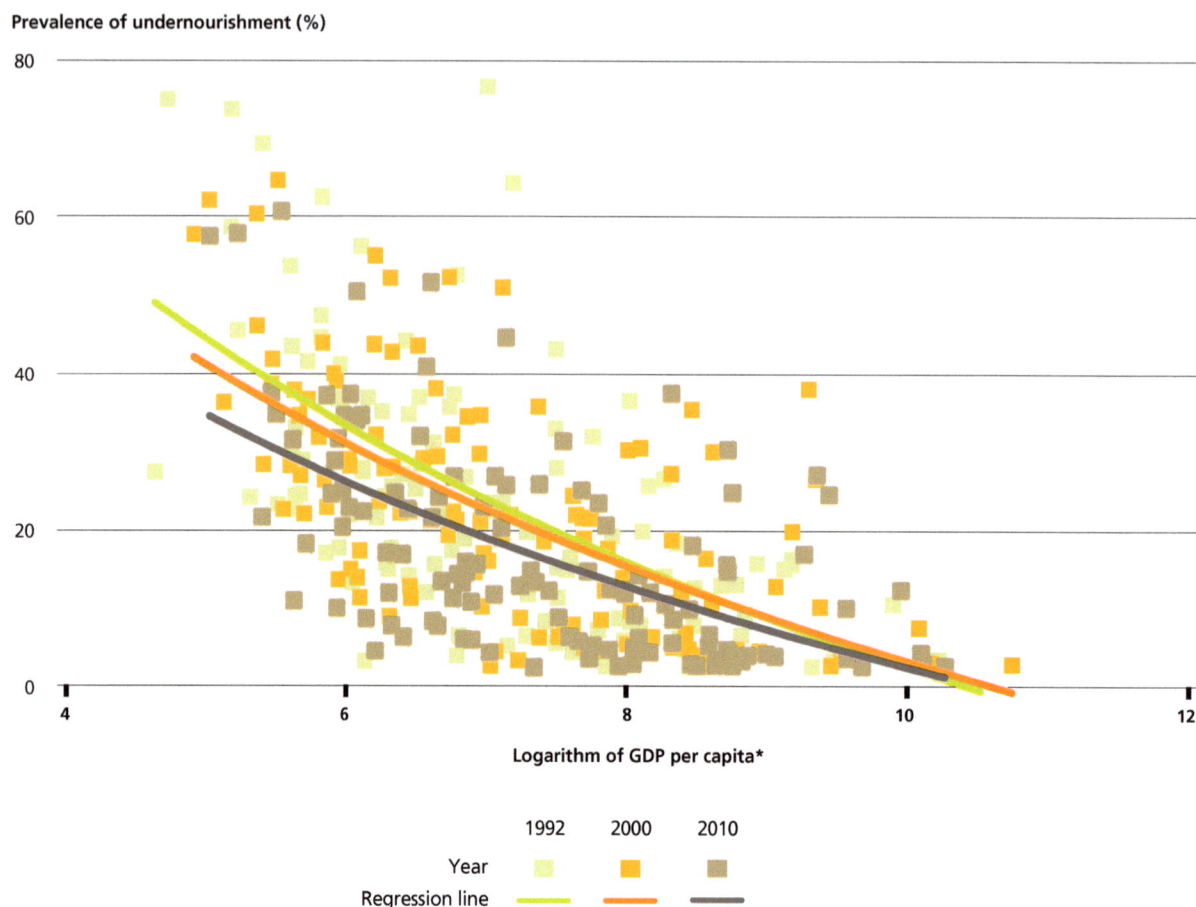

Prevalence of undernourishment (%)

*Expressed in constant 2005 US dollars.
Source: FAO and World Bank.

Not all types of growth are effective in reducing hunger and malnutrition. Very poor people cannot participate in growth processes that require capital or generate employment for the educated and skilled. For example, economic growth generated by capital-intensive exploitation of resources, such as minerals and oil, is likely to have very few or weak direct linkages to the poor. The greater the inequality in the distribution of assets, such as land, water, capital, education and health, the more difficult it is for the poor to improve their situation and the slower the progress in reducing undernourishment.[29]

Inclusive economic growth improves the incomes of the poor. If these incomes grow more rapidly than the growth rate of the economy, income distribution also improves. What matters for effectively improving food security is for economic growth to reach those in extreme poverty – the bottom quintile of the income distribution. Approximately three-quarters of the world's poor live in rural areas, with the share even higher in low-income countries.[30] In most developing regions, the risk of working poverty (workers who live on less than US$1.25 a day) is highest for employment in agriculture – about eight out of

ten working poor are engaged in vulnerable employment in the informal economy, particularly in agriculture.[31]

Agriculture on its own can trigger growth in countries with a high share of agriculture in GDP. But even if other sectors of the economy, such as mining or services, were to grow, agriculture, through targeted investments, can become an avenue through which the poor participate in the growth process. Empirical evidence suggests that agricultural growth in low-income countries is three times more effective in reducing extreme poverty compared with growth in other sectors. In sub-Saharan Africa, agricultural growth can be 11 times more effective in reducing poverty than growth in non-agricultural sectors.[32] Investments and policies that promote increased agricultural labour productivity lead to increases in rural income. Countries that have invested in their agriculture sectors – and especially in improving productivity of smallholders and family farming – have made significant progress towards the MDG 1c hunger target (Boxes 1 and 2).

Ghana: economic growth with improved food security and nutrition

Since 1990–92, Ghana has experienced high per capita economic growth rates averaging 3.3 percent per year. At the same time, the proportion of the population in extreme poverty declined from 51 percent in 1991 to 29 percent in 2005 and valid assessments suggest that the declining trend has continued. The prevalence of undernourishment – the proportion of the population experiencing chronic hunger – declined from 47.3 percent in 1990–92 to below 5 percent in 2012–14.

Agriculture has played a significant part in Ghana's growth. Together with increases in the production of cocoa, domestic food production increased significantly, promoted by policies, institutional reforms and investments under the 1991–2000 Medium-Term Agricultural Development Programme.[1]

But trade liberalization also led to substitution of local production of some staples as well as of manufacturing with imported goods, creating challenges for employment. In addition, uneven development across different population groups and regions, such as in the north of the country, led to increasing income inequality, with the Gini coefficient increasing from 38 to nearly 43 in 2005. This challenge was counterbalanced, to a significant degree, by the establishment of effective safety nets and social protection mechanisms under the country's Poverty Reduction Strategies and the National Social Protection Strategy (NSPS). The development of such social protection mechanisms was underpinned by the expansion of the tax base, brought about by rapid economic growth, from 12 to 24 percent in only 15 years, between 1990 and 2004, which doubled government revenues.

The NSPS gives priority to vulnerable women in agriculture with low education and poor credit access, while making efforts to empower other disadvantaged groups. Other programmes, such as Livelihood Empowerment Against Poverty (LEAP), which provides cash transfers to poor people with disabilities, also contributed to poverty reduction. The government, supported by the international development community, is undertaking efforts to strengthen human resources by increasing spending in education, as well as by developing the infrastructure needed to further promote growth.[2]

---

[1] S. Asuming-Brempong. 2003. *Policy Module Ghana: economic and agricultural policy reforms and their effects on the role of agriculture in Ghana*. Paper prepared for the Roles of Agriculture International Conference, 20–22 October, Rome. Rome, FAO.
[2] S.M. Sultan and T. Schrofer. 2008. *Building support to have targeted social protection interventions for the poorest: the case of Ghana*. Paper presented at the Conference on Social Protection for the Poorest in Africa: Learning from Experience, Kampala, Uganda, 8–10 September 2008.

GDP per capita and prevalence of undernourishment, Ghana, 1992–2013

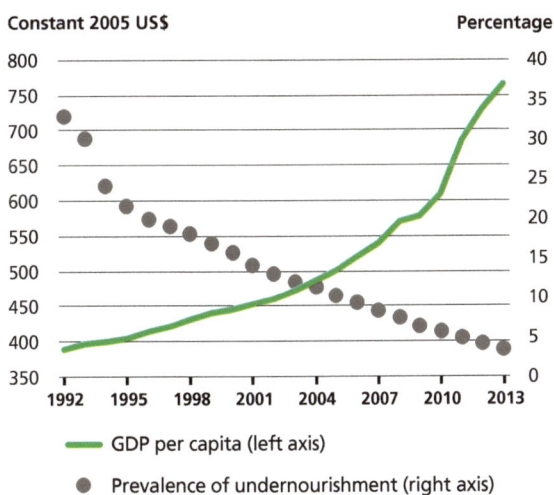

Sources: FAO and World Bank.

Food production index, Ghana, 1992–2012

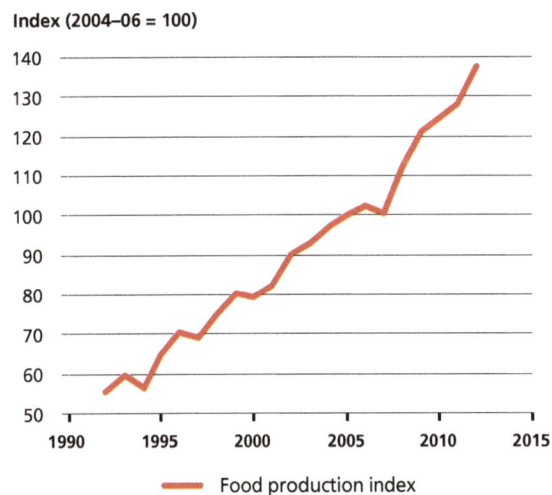

Sources: FAO and World Bank.

BOX **2**

United Republic of Tanzania: economic and agricultural growth without improved food security and nutrition

Since the beginning of the 1990s, the United Republic of Tanzania's average annual GDP growth of 2.3 percent has been mainly driven by the expansion of industry and services. Agriculture has also been expanding, but at a relatively slower pace. Between 1992 and 2013, mean annual growth in agricultural labour productivity – measured by value added per capita – averaged 1.6 percent, while the share of agriculture in GDP declined from nearly 50 percent to 26 percent.

During the same period, the country's prevalence of undernourishment increased from 24.2 percent in 1990–92 to 34.6 percent in 2012–14, and the number of undernourished from 6.4 to 17.0 million people. Only from around 2004, did the prevalence of undernourishment begin to show encouraging signs of reversing its past upward trend. Poverty remains high, although the proportion of the population living in extreme poverty declined from 72 percent to 44 percent between 1992 and 2012.

The disconnected paths between growth on the one hand, and poverty and food insecurity on the other, can be largely attributed to trade liberalization policies and privatization efforts, which were not accompanied by effective policies to modernize agriculture and include the

poor and food-insecure in the distribution of earnings from growth during the 1990s. Low investment in agriculture, which is dominated by small family farmers producing for subsistence and having poor access to local and international markets, appears to explain, at least partly, the divergence. In addition, hunger and poor nutrition constrained the productive capacity of the labour force.[1]

Even though market reforms have enhanced the role of the private sector in promoting further investments, changes in governance are still needed. The Tanzania Investment Centre, established in 2000, contributed to growth, but needs to be supported by an improved regulatory framework that can provide effective incentives for investments. In addition, the country is still missing the infrastructure needed for broad-based economic development. Secure access to land remains a key constraint, not only for agriculture, but also for domestic and foreign investors.[2]

Social protection policies have a long history in the United Republic of Tanzania and have been successful in providing income support to multiple or specific groups, and in shielding the poor and vulnerable from the impacts of shocks.[3] Nevertheless, the effectiveness of such programmes in contributing towards poverty and hunger reduction is constrained by their limited coverage and targeting exclusion errors. There will be a need to continue to expand social protection mechanisms to help reduce poverty and improve food security and nutrition.

Agricultural productivity, GDP per capita and prevalence of undernourishment, United Republic of Tanzania, 1992–2013

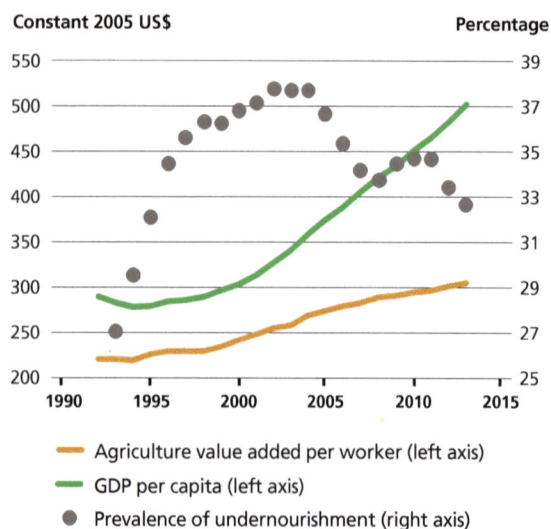

Constant 2005 US$ / Percentage

— Agriculture value added per worker (left axis)
— GDP per capita (left axis)
● Prevalence of undernourishment (right axis)

Sources: FAO and World Bank.

[1] United Republic of Tanzania, 2011. Tanzania Agriculture and Food Security Investment Plan (TAFSIP) 2011–12 to 2020–21.
[2] OECD. 2013. Overview of progress and policy challenges in Tanzania. In *OECD Investment Policy Reviews: Tanzania 2013*, pp. 23–54. Paris, OECD Publishing.
[3] F. Lerisse, D. Mmari and M. Baruani. 2003. *Vulnerability and social protection programmes in Tanzania*. Study on Social Protection Programmes on Vulnerability for the Research and Analysis Working Group.

The accommodation of gender considerations is crucial for economic growth in countries with agriculture-dependent economies. Women play important roles as producers, managers of productive resources and income earners, and they are key providers of unpaid care work in rural households and communities. However, despite decades of efforts to address gender inequalities, many rural women continue to face gender-based constraints that limit their capacity to contribute to growth and take advantage of new opportunities arising from the changes shaping national economies. This has serious consequences for well-being – not only for women themselves, but also for their families and societies at large – and it represents one of the main reasons for the economic underperformance of agriculture in poorer countries.[33] While it is sometimes argued that economic growth inevitably leads to gender equality, the empirical evidence is weak and inconsistent. Much seems to depend on policies and strategies aimed at shaping inclusive markets and reducing poverty.[34] Agriculture-based solutions need to be complemented by interventions that promote the productive potential of the

rural space. In addition, direct support to rural livelihoods through social protection programmes provides immediate relief to the most vulnerable. Such programmes also have long-term benefits – they enable broad participation of the poor in the growth process through better access to education, health and proper nutrition, all of which expand and strengthen human potential.

Social protection can establish a virtuous circle of progress involving the poor with increased incomes, employment and wages. For example, the Zero Hunger Programme and the *Bolsa Família* in Brazil were crucial for achieving inclusive growth in the country. *Bolsa Família* reached almost a quarter of the population, mainly women, transferring above US$100 every month to each family, as long as they sent their children to school.[35] With the Brazilian economy growing at 3 percent per year since 2000, thus providing the necessary public revenues, these programmes have significantly reduced income inequality – between 2000 and 2012, the average incomes of the poorest quintile of the population grew three times as fast as those of the wealthiest 20 percent.[36]

The contribution of family farming and smallholder agriculture to food security and nutrition

More than 90 percent of the 570 million farms worldwide are managed by an individual or a family, relying predominately on family labour. These farms produce more than 80 percent of the world's food, in terms of value. Globally, 84 percent of family farms are smaller than 2 hectares and manage only 12 percent of all agricultural land. While small farms tend to have higher yields than larger farms, labour productivity is less and most small family farmers are poor and food-insecure.[37] The sustainability and future food security of these farms may be threatened by intensive resource use. Public policies that recognize the diversity and complexity of the challenges faced by family farms throughout the value chain are necessary for ensuring food security.

Improved productivity of agricultural resources through sustainable intensification plays a key role in increasing food availability and improving food security and nutrition. At the global level, productivity and food availability have been increasing, contributing significantly to reductions in undernourishment worldwide. Higher agricultural labour productivity is generally associated with lower levels of undernourishment (Figure 16).

Public policies should provide incentives for the adoption of sustainable agricultural intensification practices and techniques – sustainable land management, soil conservation, improved

water management, diversified agricultural systems and agroforestry – in order to produce more outputs from the same area of land while reducing negative environmental impacts. More conventional yield-enhancing technologies, such as improved seed varieties and mineral fertilizers, are also valuable options, especially when combined with greater attention to using these inputs efficiently.

With increased productivity, farmers grow more food, become more competitive and receive higher incomes. Productivity growth in small family farms contributes to more inclusive growth, not only by reducing the prices of staple foods but also by improving access to food. With well-functioning rural labour markets, such productivity growth increases the demand for labour in rural areas, generating jobs for the poor and raising the unskilled labour wage rate. Rural household members diversify their income sources by obtaining better-paid off-farm work, which helps poverty and hunger to decline.

In spite of overall progress, marked regional differences persist. the early 1990s, average value added per worker in agriculture was lowest in sub-Saharan Africa, approximately US$700 in 2005 prices, compared with other regions, such as Eastern Asia and Latin America, where it amounted to US$4 600 and US$4 400, respectively. By 2010–13, average value added per worker in agriculture in sub-Saharan Africa

FIGURE **16**

Agricultural labour productivity and prevalence of undernourishment, 2010

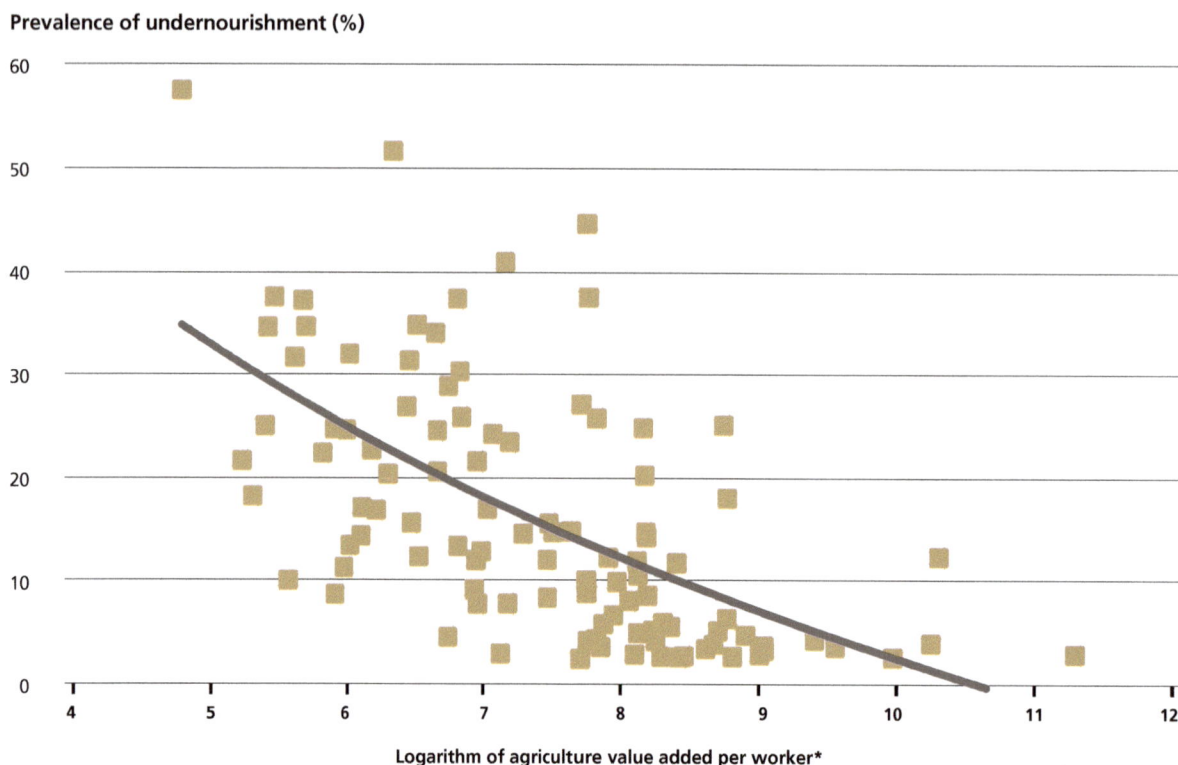

Prevalence of undernourishment (%)

Logarithm of agriculture value added per worker*

*Expressed in constant 2005 US dollars.
Source: FAO and World Bank.

amounted to US$1 199, whereas in Eastern Asia and Latin America, it had risen to US$15 300 and US$6 000, respectively. Gains in labour productivity have also been slower in sub-Saharan Africa, and so have been the reductions in the PoU, with current levels systematically higher than in other regions.

The evidence suggests that agricultural productivity gains have helped countries reduce undernourishment. For example, over the period 1990–92 to 2012–14 in sub-Saharan Africa, where agriculture is dominated by small family farms, countries that made little progress towards achieving the MDG 1c hunger target, such as Botswana, Côte d'Ivoire, Liberia, Namibia, Swaziland, Uganda, the United Republic of Tanzania and Zambia, experienced average gains in agricultural value added per worker of only 25 percent. These gains were significantly lower than those experienced in Angola, Benin, Ethiopia, Gabon, Ghana, and Mali, countries that have met the MDG 1c hunger target. On average, labour productivity in agriculture in these countries increased by 69 percent between 1990–92 and 2012–14. Over the same period, in sub-Saharan African countries that have made progress towards the target but not yet achieved it, average agricultural value added per worker increased by 42 percent.

Similar patterns are observed when looking at a more traditional measure of agricultural productivity – output per hectare. Significant yield gaps – the difference between farmers' yields and technical potential yields achieved using the latest varieties and under the best of conditions – still persist, particularly in sub-Saharan Africa. Such yield gaps reflect a largely suboptimal use of inputs and insufficient adoption of the most productive technologies. In Mali (an MDG 1c achiever), for example, the yield gap for rainfed maize – in 2008–10 – was 75 percent, a significantly high value but lower than those observed in Uganda (83 percent) and the United Republic of Tanzania (88 percent), suggesting a linkage between agricultural productivity and progress towards food security.[38]

In the recent past, in many sub-Saharan African countries, agricultural growth has been mostly driven by more extensive use of land and reallocation of productive factors – not necessarily oriented to supplying local markets and reducing food insecurity – rather than the support of public policies to expand access to agricultural credit and insurance, advisory services and sustainable technologies.

Other constraining factors that compromise agricultural productivity gains and the generation of stable incomes for family farmers include weather-related shocks; poor

transport, storage and communications infrastructure; and missing or inefficient markets. Weak institutions and inadequate public agricultural and rural development policies are major causes of such failures.

Inclusive markets for smallholders and family farmers are an important ingredient in promoting food security and nutrition. Markets not only facilitate the flow of food from surplus to deficit areas, ensuring food availability; they also transmit price signals to farmers to adjust their production and input use.[39] Well-functioning markets that foster price stability and predictability are crucial – on the one hand, a significant share of farmers rely on markets for generating part of their cash income, while, on the other hand, many family farmers are net-food buyers relying on markets to purchase part of their food needs. Smallholder and family farming productivity and access to markets are interlinked and contribute to both food availability and access to food. Improving access to marketing opportunities can also help boost productivity.

One relevant approach to increasing family farmers' access to markets is local food procurement by different levels of government (local, regional and national). Not only can public purchase schemes guarantee food security for vulnerable populations and income for smallholders and family farmers, but they may also enhance collective action to strengthen their marketing capacities and ensure greater effectiveness.

To accelerate progress in improving access to food by the poor, lagging regions, particularly sub-Saharan Africa, will increasingly have to transform their agricultural policies to significantly improve agricultural productivity and increase the quantity of food supplied by family farmers. The importance of family farming and smallholder agriculture is best reflected by the Comprehensive Africa Agriculture Development Programme (CAADP), which has established a goal of 6 percent annual agricultural growth. The expected impacts are primarily to improve food security and nutrition, reduce poverty and increase employment.

International trade and food security linkages

International trade and trade policies affect the domestic availability and prices of goods and those of the factors of production such as labour, with implications for food access. International trade can also affect market structure, productivity, sustainability of resource use, nutrition and various population groups in different ways. Assessing its impact on food security is thus highly complex. For example, banning grain exports can boost domestic supplies and reduce prices in the short run. This benefits consumers, but has negative implications for farmers producing for export. Import or export restrictions by major players affect global supplies and exacerbate price volatility at the global level. Lowering import duties reduces food prices paid by consumers, but can put pressure on the incomes of import-competing farmers, whose own food security may be negatively affected. Table 5 (p. 34) illustrates the complexity of the relationship between trade and food security by listing the possible effects of trade, both positive and negative, on different dimensions of food security. In practice, the picture is further complicated by market imperfections in national local markets, which prevent the transmission of global price changes to those markets.

■ Lessons from trade policy reforms

Policies to increase openness to international trade have generally taken place in the context of wider economic reforms, and it is therefore difficult to disentangle their effects. A number of case studies have attempted to analyse the impact of trade on food security, and, not surprisingly, the results have been mixed.[40] In China, economic reforms have generated positive results for growth, poverty reduction and food security. Trade, which has continued to grow rapidly, has played a part, although domestic reforms appear to have been more important in stimulating growth. Also in Nigeria, domestic reforms improved incentives for agricultural commodity producers, and per capita calorie intake increased substantially after the implementation of trade reforms, pointing to a possible positive impact on food security.

Similarly, in Chile, trade openness and the elimination of policy distortions stimulated both agricultural and overall economic growth and the transition from traditional crops to more profitable products for export. Research has shown that the reforms have contributed substantially to poverty reduction and food security. Peru is another example of the positive food security outcomes of institutional and economic transformations aimed at strengthening private-sector initiatives, including trade openness. However, the country implemented social protection policies and programmes, to address uneven growth across sectors and income inequality and mitigate the negative effects of the reforms on vulnerable parts of the population.

Conversely, in Guatemala, Kenya, Senegal and the United Republic of Tanzania, the food security outcomes of economic and trade reforms appear to have been disappointing. In Guatemala, while the reforms resulted in diversified production of more profitable crops, external factors (such as lower coffee prices) have undermined the

TABLE **5**

The possible effects of trade liberalization on dimensions of food security

	Possible positive effects	Possible negative effects
AVAILABILITY	Trade boosts imports and increases both the quantity and variety of food available. Dynamic effects on domestic production: Greater competition from abroad may trigger improvements in productivity through greater investment, R&D, technology spillover.	For net food-exporting countries, higher prices in international markets can divert part of production previously available for domestic consumption to exports, potentially reducing domestic availability of staple foods. For net food-importing countries, domestic producers unable to compete with imports are likely to curtail production, reducing domestic supplies and foregoing important multiplier effects of agricultural activities in rural economies.
ACCESS	For net food-importing countries, food prices typically decrease when border protection is reduced. In the competitive sectors, incomes are likely to increase as the result of greater market access for exports. Input prices are likely to decrease. The macroeconomic benefits of trade openness, such as export growth and the inflow of foreign direct investment, support growth and employment, which in turn boosts incomes.	For net food-exporting countries, the domestic prices of exportable products may increase. Employment and incomes in sensitive, import-competing sectors may decline.
UTILIZATION	A greater variety of available foods may promote more balanced diets and accommodate different preferences and tastes. Food safety and quality may improve if exporters have more advanced national control systems in place or if international standards are applied more rigorously.	Greater reliance on imported foods has been associated with increased consumption of cheaper and more readily available high-calorie/low-nutritional-value foods. Prioritization of commodity exports can divert land and resources from traditional indigenous foods that are often superior from a nutrition point of view.
STABILITY	Imports reduce the seasonal effect on food availability and consumer prices. Imports mitigate local production risks. Global markets are less prone to policy- or weather-related shocks.	For net food-importing countries, relying primarily on global markets for food supplies and open trade policies reduces the policy space to deal with shocks. Net food-importing countries may be vulnerable to changes in trade policy by exporters, such as export bans. Sectors at earlier stages of development may become more susceptible to price shocks and/or import surges.

potential to improve food security. In Kenya, limited coordination in policy sequencing seems to have slowed progress against hunger. The reforms in Senegal have shown mixed results; although the PoU declined on aggregate, female-headed households became less food-secure.

Indeed, the constraints faced by rural women, in terms of lack of access to productive factors, such as land, credit, inputs, storage and technology, may undermine their capacity to adopt new technologies and/or take advantage of economies of scale to improve their competitiveness. In several developing countries, female small farmers who are unable to compete with cheaper agricultural imports have been forced to abandon or sell their farms, which in turn can contribute to their food insecurity.[41]

While trade in itself is not intrinsically detrimental to food security, for many countries, particularly those at earlier levels of development, trade reforms can have negative effects on food security in the short-to-medium term. Recent research shows that countries supporting the primary sector tend to be better off on most dimensions of food security (food availability, access, and utilization), while taxation of this sector is detrimental to food security.[42] However, the evidence also shows that excessive support can also lead to poor performances on all dimensions of food security.

As countries become more open to international trade in agricultural products, they become more exposed and potentially more vulnerable to sudden changes in global agricultural markets. For example, import surges – sudden increases in the volume of imports from one year to the next – can hinder the development of agriculture in developing countries.

Food sectors in developing countries that are characterized by low productivity and lack of competitiveness are especially vulnerable to import surges. A sudden disruption of domestic production can have disastrous impacts on domestic farmers and workers – loss of jobs and reduced incomes, with potentially negative consequences for food security. During the period 1984–2013, China, Ecuador, India, Kenya, Nigeria, Pakistan, Uganda, the United Republic of Tanzania and Zimbabwe were prone to sudden increases in imports (defined as imports exceeding the average of the previous three years by more than 30 percent), registering more than a hundred surges.[43]

The factors that lead to an import surge may originate in the importing country itself as a result of domestic supply shortfalls or rapid increases in demand. Other factors are exogenous, for example when countries providing significant support to the production and/or export of food products channel production surpluses to the international markets.

Surges resulting from external factors can be difficult for the affected countries to manage.

Serious disruptions in domestic markets and negative food security outcomes have been used to support arguments for a more cautious approach to greater openness to agricultural trade and for the establishment of effective safeguards in new trade agreements. In circumstances where the agriculture sector has yet to play out its potential growth-enhancing role, trade policy, including trade remedies, and incentives to boost domestic production can have potentially important roles to play. At the same time, complementary policies (as in the case of Peru) can protect the most vulnerable groups from the possible negative effects of openness to trade.

■ Trade in the new agricultural markets context

The international agricultural market context has changed from one characterized by depressed and stable prices to one where market reactions to climatic and economic shocks can give rise to sudden price increases or falls. Such changes have prompted reassessment of the role of trade and trade policies in promoting food security.

As food import bills have risen significantly following increases in food prices in 2008, confidence in global markets as reliable sources of affordable food has waned, and attention has turned to support for domestic food production. As a result, some developing countries have adopted policies designed to influence domestic prices directly through border measures and price controls, or to create incentives for increasing domestic supply. Among the available trade policy instruments, export restrictions and the elimination of import tariffs have been the preferred policies to address food security concerns during periods of high and volatile prices.

Trade, in itself, is neither a threat nor a panacea when it comes to food security, but it can pose challenges and even risks that need to be considered in policy decision-making. To ensure that countries' food security and development needs are addressed in a consistent and systematic manner, they need to have a better overview of all the policy instruments available to them and the flexibility to apply the most effective policy mix for achieving their goals.

The relevance of social protection for hunger trends between 1990 and 2015

Social protection has directly contributed to hunger reduction over the MDG monitoring period. Since the late 1990s, there has been a global trend towards the extension of cash transfers and other social assistance programmes, triggered in part by the financial crises in emerging market economies during that time.[44] Social protection has since been progressively anchored in national legislation, increasing its coverage to support vulnerable groups.

Coverage has increased for many reasons, including the recognition that social protection can be instrumental in promoting sustainable and inclusive growth. Social protection is a crucial part of the policy spectrum that addresses high and persistent levels of poverty and economic insecurity, high and growing levels of inequality, insufficient investments in human resources and capabilities, and weak automatic stabilizers of aggregate demand in the face of economic shocks.

With sufficient coverage and proper implementation, social protection policies can promote both economic and social development in the short and longer term, by ensuring that people enjoy income security, have effective access to health care and other social services, are able to manage risk and are empowered to take advantage of economic opportunities. Such policies play a crucial role in fostering inclusive and sustainable growth, strengthening domestic demand, facilitating the structural transformation of national economies, and promoting decent work.[45]

Between 1990 and 2015, social protection programmes have grown exponentially. Although much of this increase occurred in high- and middle-income countries, significant progress in social protection coverage has also been made in the developing regions, as for example in Africa, through innovative cash transfer and health-care programmes.[46] Today, every country in the world has at least one social assistance programme in place. School-feeding programmes – the most widespread type of social protection programme – are implemented in 130 countries. Unconditional cash transfers are also common, and are now implemented in 118 countries globally. Likewise, conditional cash transfer and public works/community asset programmes continue to expand rapidly.[47] Global and regional efforts have also been instrumental, including the push for national social protection floors endorsed by International Labour Organization (ILO) Recommendation 202.[48] Yet, despite the proliferation of programmes around the world, the ILO estimates that 70 percent of the world's poor still do not have access to adequate social protection.[49]

International organizations, such as FAO and WFP, play important roles in designing and implementing efficient and effective safety net programmes and social protection systems in the countries with a focus on food security and nutrition. Social protection systems often meet immediate food gap needs and, if designed accordingly, they can help improve lives and livelihoods – a key factor for reducing the number of hungry people in the world.

Recent research concludes that approximately 150 million people worldwide are prevented from falling into extreme poverty thanks to social protection.[50] However, the impact of social assistance programmes such as cash transfers on well-being extends beyond the direct effects of transfers. Transfers can help households manage risk and mitigate the impact of shocks that keep households mired in poverty.

Social assistance programmes such as cash transfer programmes can influence the productive capacity of beneficiaries, in particular those with limited access to financial services for investment and risk mitigation. The provision of regular and predictable cash transfers brings significant benefits when markets are missing or do not function well. When transfers are of sufficient size and combined with additional support to beneficiaries, they can often be saved and/or invested in productive assets and can improve social inclusion for even greater returns over the participants' lifetimes.[51] In combination with savings and credit, environmental rehabilitation and agricultural insurance, transfers can encourage prudent risk-taking and increase productive outcomes – even for the poorest households.[52]

BOX **3**

The Productive Safety Net Programme in Ethiopia

Established in 2005, the Productive Safety Net Programme (PSNP) is designed to enable the rural poor facing chronic food insecurity to resist shocks, create assets and become food self-sufficient. The programme provides predictable multi-annual transfers, as food, cash or a combination of both, to help chronically food-insecure people survive food-deficit periods and avoid depleting their productive assets while attempting to meet their basic food requirements.

The combination of cash and food transfers is based on season and need, with food given primarily during the lean season between June and August. Vulnerable households receive six months of assistance each year to protect them from acute food insecurity. Able-bodied members of households participating in the programme are required to contribute to productive activities that will build more resilient livelihoods, such as rehabilitating land and water resources and developing community infrastructure, including rehabilitating rural roads and building schools and clinics.

Studies have shown that PSNP has had a positive impact on the livelihoods of participating households. On average, across the regions in which the programme operates (Afar, Amhara, Dire Dawa, Harare, Oromiya, SNNP, Somali and Tigray), its predictable transfers have shortened the lean season, during which the rural poor are most food-insecure, by over one month – the most significant improvement took place in Amhara, where the lean season was shortened by nearly two months. The programme also contributed towards increasing children's access to food. During the lean seasons between 2006 and 2010, the average number of meals consumed by children in targeted households rose by 15 percent.

In some cases, the longer a household participates in the programme, the shorter the lean period can become. This is because regular and predictable cash transfers lead to increased on-farm investments and improve the productive capacity of beneficiary households. On average, five years of participation raises livestock holdings each year by 0.38 tropical livestock units, a weighted aggregation of different kinds of livestock. In Oromiya, beneficiary households experienced an increase in the value of productive assets of 112 birr.

Poverty and prevalence of undernourishment, Ethiopia, 1992–2013

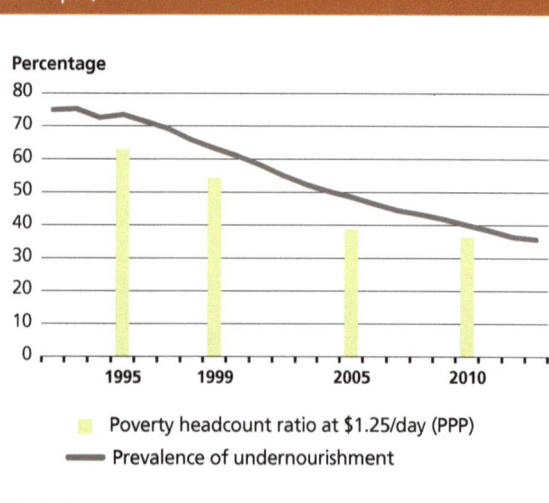

Percentage

- ▢ Poverty headcount ratio at $1.25/day (PPP)
- — Prevalence of undernourishment

Sources: FAO and World Bank.

Source: G. Berhane, J. Hoddinott, N. Kumar and A.S. Taffesse. 2011. *The impact of Ethiopia's productive safety nets and household asset building programme: 2006–2010.* Washington, DC, International Food Policy Research Institute.

Social assistance programmes, particularly when combined with additional interventions in the areas of drinking water supply, health and/or education, have been shown to enhance nutritional outcomes and promote human capital. The integration of nutrition objectives into social assistance programmes also has the potential to significantly accelerate progress in reducing undernutrition and raising economic productivity.[53] Furthermore, women are direct beneficiaries of many social assistance programmes, such as cash transfers. With more control of resources, this has empowered them with positive impacts on food security and nutritional status, especially of children.[54] However, such positive outcomes depend on other contextual factors and require complementary interventions.

Over the past twenty five years, evidence has emerged that social protection programmes can play a significant role in achieving food security and nutrition targets. The evidence suggests that increasing spending for strengthened social protection programmes can be a highly cost-effective way to promote rural poverty reduction and improved food security and nutrition, and, hence, to achieve development goals.[55] The fact that, despite the rapid growth of social protection programmes in recent decades, about 70 percent of the world population still lacks access to more adequate, formal forms of social security, indicates there is still considerable need for expanded coverage and, hence, scope for accelerating the eradication of hunger. However, just expanding social protection programmes will not suffice. The most effective social protection policies for improved food security and rural poverty reduction have been those that are well integrated with agriculture sector policies and fully aligned with the priorities and vision set out in broader strategies aimed at creating viable and sustainable livelihoods for the poor.

Protracted crises and hunger

Countries and areas in protracted crisis are "environments in which a significant proportion of the population is acutely vulnerable to death, disease and disruption of livelihoods over a prolonged period of time. Governance in these environments is usually very weak, with the state having limited capacity to respond to, and mitigate, threats to the population, or to provide adequate levels of protection."[56] Based on the criteria set out in *The State of Food Insecurity in the World 2010*,[57] the list of countries considered to be in protracted crisis situations was updated in 2012 to encompass 20 countries[58]. However, it should be noted that some protracted crisis situations are limited to specific geographic areas, and may not affect the entire country, let alone the entire population.

Although protracted crises are diverse in both their causes and effects, food insecurity and malnutrition are common prevalent features.[59] Food insecurity and malnutrition are particularly severe, persistent and widespread in protracted crisis contexts. The approximate combined population in protracted crisis situations in 2012 was 366 million people, of whom approximately 129 million were undernourished between 2010 and 2012 (including conservative estimates for countries lacking data). This accounted for approximately 19 percent of the global total of food-insecure people. In 2012, the mean prevalence of undernourishment in protracted crisis situations was 39 percent, compared with 15 percent, on average, in the rest of the developing world (see Figure 17).

Achieving the MDG 1c target of halving the proportion of undernourished population in these countries poses an enormous challenge. Of the 20 countries in protracted crisis identified above, only one, Ethiopia, has reached the MDG 1c target. All the others report either insufficient progress or even deterioration.

FIGURE **17**

Food insecurity: are protracted crises different?

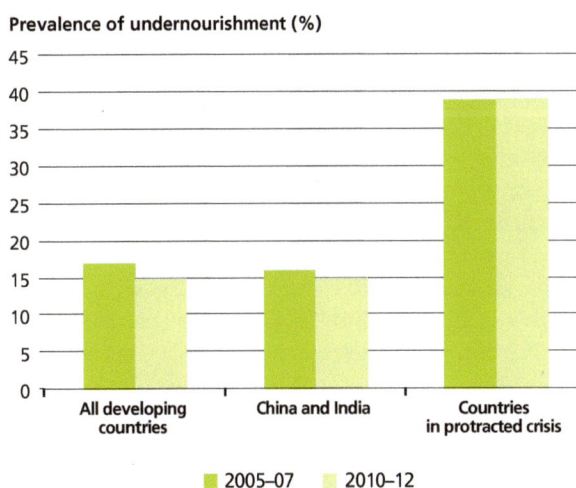

Prevalence of undernourishment (%)

2005–07   2010–12

Source: FAO.

◼ The typology of crises

Over the past 30 years, the typology of crises has gradually evolved from catastrophic, short-term, acute and highly visible events to more structural, longer-term and protracted situations resulting from a combination of multiple contributing factors, especially natural disasters and conflicts, with climate change, financial and price crises increasingly frequent among the exacerbating factors. In other words, protracted crises have become the new norm, while acute short-term crises are now the exception. Indeed, more crises are considered protracted today than in the past.[60]

From a food security and nutrition perspective, in 1990, only 12 countries in Africa were facing food crises, of which only four were in protracted crisis. Just 20 years later, a total of 24 countries were facing food crises, with 19 of these having been in crisis for eight or more of the previous ten years.[61] Moreover, the growing imperative of dealing with the long-term contexts of these emergencies is becoming evident. For instance, the Bosphorus Compact[62] reported that global humanitarian appeals between 2004 and 2013 increased by 446 percent overall – rising from US$3 billion to US$16.4 billion. Similarly, the number of displaced people at the end of 2013 was 51.2 million, more than at any point since the end of World War Two. The average length of displacement in major refugee situations is now 20 years. And nine out of ten humanitarian appeals continue for more than three years, with 78 percent of spending by the Organisation for Economic Co-operation and Development's Development Assistance Committee donors allocated to protracted emergencies.

Over the past three decades, the causes of crises have become more interconnected, displaying an evolving trend of triggers for protracted crises due to natural causes, either human-induced, or stemming from a combination of human and natural causes.[63] Conflicts are increasingly the main underlying cause, with the prevalence of human-induced conflicts higher than previously. As such, conflicts are now a common feature of crises. The complex relation between conflict and food security and nutrition is still to be fully explored (Box 4).

BOX **4**

Conflict and political instability

Food insecurity can be a direct result of violent conflict and political instability as well as an exacerbating factor. On the one hand, food insecurity is among the factors that can trigger and/or deepen conflict, often due to underlying economic and structural factors. For instance, sudden and unforeseen food price rises, or the reduction or removal of subsidies on basic foodstuffs, can be a catalyst for civil and political unrest, as in the social upheaval and political violence of the Arab Spring in 2011 when governments in the Near East reduced subsidies for bread. Natural disasters, drought and famine can also contribute to political unrest and violent conflict, as evidenced by the Sahel and West Africa region. Food insecurity can exacerbate political instability and violent conflict when specific groups are economically marginalized, services are distributed inequitably or where there is competition over scarce natural resources needed for food security. Periodic conflicts between farmers and herders in the semi-arid Sahel and East Africa regions illustrate this.[1]

On the other hand, mortality caused by conflict due to food insecurity and famine can far exceed deaths caused directly by violence. Conflict disrupts livelihoods in rural and urban areas, and undermines smallholder agricultural productivity; it is a leading cause of hunger and undermines food security and nutrition in multiple ways. All situations of extreme food insecurity and famine in the Horn of Africa since the 1980s have been characterized by conflict in some form, transforming food security crises into devastating famines. Globally, between 2004 and 2009, around 55 000 people lost their lives each year as a direct result of conflict or terrorism.[2] In contrast, famine caused by conflict and drought resulted in the deaths of more than 250 000 people in Somalia alone between 2010 and 2012.[3]

Figures from ongoing conflicts and political instability reinforce this link. In Iraq, food prices are high and volatile in conflict-affected governorates, with the food basket costing 25–30 percent more than in the capital Baghdad.[4] Stressed crop conditions are clearly visible through satellite imaging, which confirms the negative impact of the conflict on irrigation, availability of agricultural inputs and access to fields. In Palestine, displacement, livelihood disruption and increasing unemployment has led to a recent deterioration in food security. In 2013, 33 percent of all Palestinians were considered to be food-insecure (19 percent in the West Bank and 57 percent in the Gaza Strip), with a further 16 percent considered to be particularly vulnerable to becoming food-insecure.[5] At the start of 2015, as a result of continuing violence, civil unrest and fragmentation in the Syrian Arab Republic, coupled with international sanctions, disrupted food production and hikes in domestic fuel and food prices, 9.8 million people required various levels of food, agriculture and livelihood-related assistance. Of these, 6.8 million people were in critical need of food assistance.[6]

In South Sudan, between January and March 2015, some 2.5 million people were facing Crisis (IPC Phase 3) or Emergency (IPC Phase 4) levels of food insecurity[7] as the

■ Ways in which crises impact food security

Protracted crises undermine food security and nutrition in multiple ways, affecting the availability, access and utilization of food. Disruptions to crop production, livestock rearing and trade can have a negative impact on food availability. People's access to food is frequently affected in crises because of displacement, disruptions to livelihoods, or when land is taken. For example, when state and customary institutions are unable or unwilling to protect and promote individuals' legal rights, attempts to take land from women, orphans and other vulnerable individuals go unchecked.[64] Finally, the utilization of food can be impacted by changes in intra-household and community relations and power dynamics and by inequitable service delivery.

Food insecurity can be further deepened and self-perpetuating as people use up their reserves of food, finance and other assets, and turn to unsustainable coping mechanisms, such as selling off productive assets and taking up activities that lead to land degradation to meet immediate food needs.

Gender and age are two powerful determinants of the impact of protracted crises on individuals. Women are more likely than men to be affected and their access to aid can be undermined by gender-based discrimination. Pre-existing gender-based disparities in access to assets such as land, property or credit mean that women have often fewer financial resources than men to cope with impacts such as loss of productive capacity, leaving them unable to afford the increased prices of food in crisis-affected areas.[65] Protracted crises have also been found to put additional care burdens on women post-crisis, while limited mobility and work opportunities outside the home reduce their range of coping strategies. Often, with male household members absent, due to death, migration or recruitment into armed forces, women are not always able to claim family assets, such as land, livestock, tools and machinery, previously owned by their husbands, especially if they are illiterate or insufficiently aware of their legal rights with significant negative implications for food security.

conflict had displaced populations, reduced food production and disrupted markets.[8] It is worth noting that prior to the eruption of conflict in December 2013, no one in South Sudan was in IPC Phase 4. The immediate effects of the conflict on the food security situation were highlighted by the revised IPC analysis in May 2014, which reported some 3.5 million people in IPC Phases 3 and 4, of which more than 1 million were facing Emergency (Phase 4) level.[9] Similarly, the conflict in the Central African Republic has exacerbated food insecurity. In April–May 2014, IPC estimated (although with limited confidence) that roughly 1.7 million people were severely food-insecure (IPC Phases 3 and 4).[10] This was a sharp increase from 900 000 people estimated in November 2013, prior to the outbreak of conflict.

In all these examples, it is likely that the major causes of current food insecurity will persist for some time, with households increasingly adopting short-term coping and survival strategies that can render livelihoods unsustainable and jeopardise future prospects, for example selling productive assets such as livestock, or remaining heavily reliant on food assistance. In such contexts, progress towards the MDG 1c target in these countries is likely to be extremely difficult to achieve.

[1] M. Moritz. 2012. *Farmer-herder conflicts in sub-Saharan Africa* (available at http://www.eoearth.org/view/article/51cbedc67896bb431f693d72).

[2] Geneva Declaration on Armed Violence and Development. 2011. *Global Burden of Armed Violence 2011: Lethal encounters*. Geneva, Switzerland, Geneva Declaration Secretariat; IFAD. 2011. *IFAD Guidelines for Disaster Early Recovery* (EB 2011/102/R.29). Rome; and IFAD. 2006. *IFAD Policy on Crisis Prevention and Recovery* (EB 2006/87/R.3/Rev.1). Rome.

[3] FAO. 2013. *Study suggests 258 000 Somalis died due to severe food insecurity and famine*. News release (available at http://www.fao.org/somalia/news/detail-events/en/c/247642/).

[4] WFP. 2015. *Global food security update*. Issue 17, March 2015 (available at http://documents.wfp.org/stellent/groups/public/documents/ena/wfp272750.pdf).

[5] Food Security Cluster. 2014. *Food insecurity in Palestine remains high*. Socio-Economic and Food Security (SEFSec) High Level Statement, June 2014 (available at http://foodsecuritycluster.net/document/sefsec-high-level-statement-june-2014).

[6] WFP. 2014. *Syrian Arab Republic: Highlights as of December 2014*. Food security analysis website (available at http://vam.wfp.org/CountryPage_overview.aspx?iso3=SYR).

[7] The Integrated Food Security Phase Classification (IPC) scale categorizes the severity of acute food insecurity into five phases, from "1 –Minimal" to "5 – Famine", each with distinct implications for proactive decision-making regarding appropriate and effective response (see http://www.ipcinfo.org/ipcinfo-home/en/).

[8] IPC. 2015. *South Sudan – 2.5 million people in either Crisis or Emergency between January and March 2015*. News release (available at http://www.ipcinfo.org/ipcinfo-detail-forms/ipcinfo-news-detail/en/c/276738/).

[9] IPC. 2014. South Sudan communication summary (available at http://www.ipcinfo.org/fileadmin/user_upload/ipcinfo/docs/IPC_SouthSudan_Sept%202014_Communication_Summary.pdf).

[10] IPC. 2014. *IPC Alert: Central African Republic calls for immediate actions to avoid a worsening emergency situation*. Web alert (available at http://www.ipcinfo.org/ipcinfo-detail-forms/ipcinfo-news-detail/en/c/232629/).

BOX 5

Threats of natural disasters and climate change to food security

Exposure to natural hazards and disasters is a major cause of food insecurity, a problem exacerbated by climate change. Between 2003 and 2013, natural hazards and disasters in the developing regions affected more than 1.9 billion people and resulted in nearly half a trillion US dollars in estimated damage. Through a review of post-disaster needs assessments in 48 developing countries, FAO estimated that the agriculture sector absorbs approximately 22 percent of the total economic impact of these disasters,[1] clearly affecting the capacity of the sector to support food security.

Small island developing states (SIDS) are at particular risk.[2] The World Bank estimates that SIDS countries account for two-thirds of the countries incurring the highest relative losses due to natural disasters each year. In the Pacific Islands region alone, infrastructure, buildings and cash crops with an estimated value of US$112 billion are considered to be at risk of natural disasters.[3] In the Caribbean, annual damage to infrastructure from natural disasters is estimated between US$0.5 to 1.0 billion.[4]

Climate change multiplies the risks of natural hazards, through altered rainfall and temperature patterns as well as increased frequency and intensity of extreme events such as drought and flooding.[5] The Fifth Assessment Report of the Intergovernmental Panel on Climate Change, released in 2014, noted that climate change is already having a negative impact on agriculture, affecting major crops, livestock production and fisheries. These tropical areas of high exposure to climate change are also characterized by high food insecurity.

When disasters strike, they have immediate repercussions on the livelihoods and food security of millions of family farmers and smallholders, pastoralists, fishers and forest-dependent communities in developing countries where agriculture employs from 30 to over 80 percent of the population. Considering only the impacts of major events for a limited number of countries over the 2003–13 period, estimates of losses were about US$13 billion for the crop sector, mainly due to flooding and storm damage and US$11 billion for livestock, principally attributable to drought, and these are only a small fraction of the total costs actually incurred.[6]

Natural disasters also have a wide and complex range of indirect effects on food security. Greater uncertainty and higher risks reduce the incentives to invest in agricultural production, particularly for family farmers and smallholders with limited or no access to credit and insurance.[7] Greater emphasis on low-risk, but low-returning production activities, and lowered levels of fixed and operating capital inputs, generally lead to both lower current and future farm profits. Natural disasters also give rise to reductions in food consumption, education

and healthcare, which, in turn, can lead to long-term losses in terms of income generation and future food security. In the United Republic of Tanzania, for example, crop shocks going back to 1991–95 provoked consumption growth losses of between 17 and 40 percent in 2004.[8]

Taken together, exposure to natural disasters, exacerbated by climate change, can pose significant challenges to countries in their progress towards the international hunger targets. Reducing vulnerability to natural hazards and climate change requires a comprehensive strategy to minimize risk exposure while maximizing effective responses. This includes increasing the resilience of agro-ecosystems through sustainable land management approaches, together with programmes to enhance socio-economic resilience such as social protection, improved agricultural market governance and value chain development, as well as insurance programmes and effective early warning systems. Resilience-building is specific to local conditions and thus capacity to identify and implement strategies at local level is key.

Empirical evidence from various countries has shown that implementing disaster risk-reduction measures can produce long-term benefits – from reduced future losses to more resilient livelihoods and productive agro-ecosystems. Countries such as Bangladesh, Cuba, Madagascar and Viet Nam have been able to reduce drastically the impact of weather related hazards, such as tropical storms and floods, through improved early warning systems and other disaster-preparedness and risk-reduction measures.[9]

[1] FAO. 2015. *The impact of natural hazards and disasters on agriculture and food and nutrition security: a call for action to build resilient livelihoods*. Rome.
[2] FAO. 2015. *Food security and nutrition in Small Island Developing States*. Rome.
[3] World Bank. 2012. *Acting today for tomorrow: a policy and practice note for climate- and disaster- resilient development in the Pacific Islands region*. Washington, DC.
[4] World Bank. 2013. *Building resilience: integrating climate and disaster risk into development: lessons from World Bank Group experience*. Washington, DC.
[5] IPCC, 2014: Summary for policymakers. In: IPCC. *Climate Change 2014: impacts, adaptation, and vulnerability*. Contribution of Working Group II to the Fifth Assessment Report of the Intergovernmental Panel on Climate Change, pp. 1–32. Cambridge, UK and New York, USA, Cambridge University Press.
[6] Op cit., see note 1.
[7] J.R. Porter, L. Xie, A.J. Challinor, K. Cochrane, S.M. Howden, M.M. Iqbal, D.B. Lobell and M.I. Travasso. 2014. Food security and food production systems. In: IPCC. *Climate Change 2014: impacts, adaptation, and vulnerability*. Contribution of Working Group II to the Fifth Assessment Report of the Intergovernmental Panel on Climate Change, pp. 485–533. Cambridge, UK and New York, USA, Cambridge University Press.
[8] K. Beegle, J. de Weerdt and S. Dercon. 2008. Adult mortality and consumption growth in the age of HIV/AIDS. *Economic Development and Cultural Change*, 56(2): 299–326.
[9] United Nations. 2010. *Keeping the promise: united to achieve the Millennium Development Goals*. New York, USA.

■ Why is it so difficult to deal with food insecurity and malnutrition in protracted crises?

Addressing food insecurity and malnutrition in protracted crises is particularly challenging. Evidence shows that stakeholders need to address the critical manifestations of protracted crises, such as hunger and malnutrition, and disruption to and depletion of livelihoods, while simultaneously addressing underlying causes such as poor governance, inadequate capacities, limited access to scarce natural resources and conflict.

In addition, policies and actions have to consider the specific features and complex challenges presented by protracted crises, including their longevity; the particular need to protect marginalized and vulnerable groups, and to respect basic human rights; the mismatch between short-term funding mechanisms and long-term needs, and how best to integrate humanitarian and development assistance; the often poor coordination of responses; and inadequate ownership by national stakeholders of response-related

processes. Finally, the context specificity of protracted crises makes it difficult, and undesirable, to adopt "one-size-fits-all" approaches.

Nonetheless, examples exist of good practices in addressing some of the issues at the root of protracted crises, ranging from innovative funding mechanisms such as crisis modifiers, to more comprehensive country owned processes (see Box 6 for more details). In addition, rural women should be seen as partners in the rehabilitation process rather than simply "victims". Indeed, evidence indicates that relief programmes that adopt a gender perspective can avert widespread malnutrition and lead to quick and more extensive recovery in food production and other aspects of livelihoods.[66]

Protracted crises are becoming an increasingly important global problem, negatively impacting on people's food security and nutrition, and often the result of instability and conflict. Successful experiences exist, but need to be scaled up, which requires a high degree of political commitment at all levels (see Box 7). Current efforts by the Committee on World Food Security (CFS) to finalize a Framework for Action for Food Security and Nutrition in Protracted Crises could be

---

BOX **6**

Crisis modifiers as innovative financing mechanisms

Crisis modifiers are budget lines in longer-term interventions that can quickly shift programmatic objectives towards mitigation of a crisis without going through the lengthy process of fund-raising and proposal writing. This mechanism enables a more integrated, agile and flexible approach that can reduce the erosion of development gains in times of crisis while responding to immediate needs. As such, it is a valuable approach to sequencing and integrating humanitarian and development assistance around the shared goal of building resilience. This approach was pioneered by the United States Agency for International Development (USAID) / Office of United States Foreign Disaster Assistance (OFDA) in Ethiopia to shift development funding to deliver immediate, life-saving interventions in response to the 2011 drought.

Shift toward comprehensive risk management
A range of sophisticated risk management models at continental, national and community levels are being rolled out to provide contingency funding to governments and insurance to farmers in the event of a severe drought or other natural disasters. The African Risk Capacity (ARC) is one such example. ARC is a novel partnership, between the African Union, UN agencies, philanthropic foundations

and aid providers, which aims to be an "… Africa-owned, standalone financial entity that will provide African governments with timely, reliable and cost-effective contingency funding in the event of a severe drought by pooling risks across the continent".[1] ARC translates country-specific rainfall data into an approximate "response cost". Countries pay premiums, based on probable risks, to an index-based insurance mechanism – thus pooling the risk of drought across several countries and taking advantage of the weather system diversity across Africa. There are analogous community-level systems such the R4 Rural Resilience Initiative in Ethiopia and Senegal to support resilience to climate variability and shocks. Insurance and other innovative financing mechanisms are not stand-alone solutions, but elements that should be considered as part of a more comprehensive package that reduces risks, supports livelihoods and protects assets in crisis situations.

---

[1] African Union and WFP. 2012. *African Risk Capacity (ARC) briefing book* (available at http://www.africanriskcapacity.org/c/document_library/get_file?uuid=9fb04f73-f7c4-47ea-940f-ebe275f55767&groupId=350251).

BOX 7

Addressing food security and nutrition issues in protracted crisis situations: success story

Successful interventions in addressing food security and nutrition issues in protracted crisis situations are often seen to be more about preventive actions than responses to the impacts of recurrent crises. One positive country example in dealing with recurrent food security crises is Ethiopia, which recently reached the MDG 1c hunger target.

The positive results can be attributed to several interlinked factors: first, an unprecedented GDP annual growth rate of 10 percent, and second, a political shift from humanitarian and emergency interventions towards longer-term interventions aimed at dealing with the structural causes of hunger, vulnerability and poverty in the most vulnerable and resource-depleted areas of the country. Until 2005, short-term, mainly food-aid-driven responses were the standard response to such events. Since 2005, the Government has implemented a widespread social protection programme, the Productive Safety Net Programme (PSNP). This reaches some 7.5 million vulnerable people through a cash/food-for-work approach. The added value is that, while providing the most vulnerable groups with adequate entitlements to access food, it also enables them to combat the structural causes of food insecurity, for example by improving agricultural activities and investing in rural infrastructure.

Key findings

- **Economic growth is necessary for sustaining progress in efforts to reduce poverty, hunger and malnutrition. But it is not sufficient.**

- **Inclusive growth – growth that provides opportunities for those with meagre assets, skills and opportunities – improves the incomes and livelihoods of the poor, and is effective in the fight against hunger and malnutrition. Rural people make up a high percentage of the hungry and malnourished in developing countries, and efforts to promote growth in agriculture and the rural sector can be an important component of a strategy for promoting inclusive growth and improving food security and nutrition.**

- **Improving the productivity of resources held by family farmers and smallholders is, in most cases, an essential element of inclusive growth and has broad implications for the livelihoods of the rural poor and for the rural economy in general. Well-functioning markets for food, inputs and labour can help to integrate family farmers and smallholders in the rural economy and enable the rural poor to diversify their livelihoods, which is critical for managing risk, and reducing hunger and malnutrition.**

- **In many situations, international trade openness has an important potential for improving food security and nutrition by increasing food availability and for promoting investment and growth. International trade agreements should provide for effective safeguards and greater policy space for developing countries to avoid detrimental effects on domestic food security and nutrition.**

- **Social protection directly contributes to the reduction of hunger and malnutrition by promoting income security and access to better nutrition, healthcare and education. By increasing human capacities and mitigating the impact of shocks, social protection fosters the ability of the very poor to participate in the growth process through better access to decent employment.**

- **Prevalence of food insecurity and malnutrition is significantly higher in protracted crisis contexts resulting from conflict and natural disasters. Strong political commitment is necessary to address the root causes of protracted crises situations. Action should focus on addressing vulnerability, respecting basic human rights and integrating humanitarian and development assistance.**

TABLE A1
Prevalence of undernourishment and progress towards the World Food Summit (WFS)[1] and the Millennium Development Goal (MDG)[2] targets in developing regions

Regions/subregions/countries	Number of people undernourished							Proportion of undernourished in total population						
	1990–92	2000–02	2005–07	2010–12	2014–16[3]	Change so far[4]	Progress towards WFS target[5]	1990–92	2000–02	2005–07	2010–12	2014–16[3]	Change so far[4]	Progress towards MDG target[5]
	(millions)					(%)		(%)						
WORLD	1 010.6	929.6	942.3	820.7	794.6	−21.4		18.6	14.9	14.3	11.8	10.9	−41.6	
Developed regions	20.0	21.2	15.4	15.7	14.7	−26.3		<5.0	<5.0	<5.0	<5.0	<5.0	na	
Developing regions	990.7	908.4	926.9	805.0	779.9	−21.3	◄►	23.3	18.2	17.3	14.1	12.9	−44.5	○
Least-developed countries[6]	209.3	244.3	237.6	237.8	250.9	19.9	▲	40.0	36.5	31.4	27.7	26.7	−33.2	●
Landlocked developing countries[7]	94.4	112.3	105.2	103.8	107.4	13.8	▲	35.6	33.6	28.1	24.1	22.7	−36.1	●
Small island developing states[8]	10.2	10.7	10.8	9.7	10.1	−0.5	◄►	24.5	22.5	21.3	18.2	18.0	−26.3	●
Low-income economies[9]	199.2	238.4	231.5	236.6	247.6	24.3	▲	39.1	36.6	31.8	28.7	27.5	−29.7	●
Lower-middle-income economies[10]	407.7	374.5	420.0	353.2	355.6	−12.8	◄►	22.8	17.5	18.2	14.2	13.5	−40.7	●
Low-income food-deficit countries[11]	460.2	468.9	512.8	474.0	495.8	7.7	▲	27.6	22.8	22.7	19.2	18.8	−32.0	●
FAO regions														
Africa[12]	175.7	203.6	206.0	205.7	220.0	25.2	▲	33.2	30.0	26.5	24.1	23.2	−30.1	●
Asia and the Pacific[13]	726.2	617.2	645.3	525.4	490.1	−32.5	◄►	24.3	18.0	17.8	13.7	12.3	−49.5	●
Europe and Central Asia[14]	9.9	11.5	8.8	7.2	5.9	−40.3	◄►	8.0	8.5	6.2	<5.0	<5.0	na	●
Latin America and the Caribbean[15]	66.1	60.3	47.1	38.3	34.3	−48.0	✳	14.7	11.4	8.4	6.4	5.5	−62.7	●
Near East and North Africa[16]	16.5	23.1	27.3	33.9	33.0	99.8	▲	6.6	7.5	8.1	8.3	7.5	14.6	●
AFRICA	181.7	210.2	213.0	218.5	232.5	27.9	▲	27.6	25.4	22.7	20.7	20.0	−27.7	●
Northern Africa[17]	6.0	6.6	7.0	5.1	4.3	−27.9	◄►	<5.0	<5.0	<5.0	<5.0	<5.0	na	●
Algeria	2.1	2.7	2.3	ns	ns	>−50.0	▼	7.7	8.4	6.8	<5.0	<5.0	na	●
Egypt	ns	ns	ns	ns	ns	>−50.0	◄►	<5.0	<5.0	<5.0	<5.0	<5.0	na	●
Morocco	1.5	1.9	1.7	1.7	ns	>0.0	▲	5.9	6.6	5.5	5.2	<5.0	na	●
Tunisia	ns	ns	ns	ns	ns	>−50.0	▼	<5.0	<5.0	<5.0	<5.0	<5.0	na	●
Sub-Saharan Africa[18]	175.7	203.6	206.0	205.7	220.0	25.2	▲	33.2	30.0	26.5	24.1	23.2	−30.1	●
Eastern Africa	103.9	121.6	122.5	118.7	124.2	19.6	▲	47.2	43.1	37.8	33.7	31.5	−33.2	●
Djibouti	0.5	0.4	0.3	0.2	0.1	−68.8	✳	74.8	48.9	33.0	22.0	15.9	−78.8	●
Ethiopia	37.3	37.3	34.3	32.1	31.6	−15.1	◄►	74.8	54.8	43.8	36.0	32.0	−57.2	●
Kenya	7.9	10.4	10.4	10.0	9.9	26.0	▲	32.4	32.3	28.2	23.8	21.2	−34.5	●
Madagascar	3.3	5.8	6.6	6.9	8.0	146.0	▲	27.3	35.6	34.9	31.7	33.0	21.0	●
Malawi	4.3	3.1	3.5	3.3	3.6	−16.8	◄►	44.7	27.0	26.4	21.3	20.7	−53.7	●
Mauritius	<0.1	<0.1	<0.1	ns	ns	>−50.0	◄►	8.1	6.7	5.4	<5.0	<5.0	na	●
Mozambique	7.8	7.9	8.0	7.3	6.9	−12.3	◄►	56.1	42.1	36.9	29.9	25.3	−54.9	●
Rwanda	3.9	4.7	4.5	3.9	3.9	2.0	▲	55.6	54.3	46.4	35.4	31.6	−43.1	○
Sudan (former)[19]	10.6	9.6	10.2	na	na	na		40.0	27.2	25.0	na	na	na	
Uganda	4.2	7.1	6.6	8.7	10.3	143.2	▲	23.2	28.1	22.3	24.8	25.5	10.1	●
United Republic of Tanzania	6.4	13.0	14.1	16.1	16.8	163.8	▲	24.2	37.1	35.4	34.7	32.1	32.9	●
Zambia	2.7	4.7	6.0	6.9	7.4	173.1	▲	33.8	45.4	50.7	50.3	47.8	41.4	●
Zimbabwe	4.6	5.5	5.1	4.5	5.0	9.4	▲	42.7	43.7	40.4	33.5	33.4	−21.9	●
Middle Africa	24.2	42.4	47.7	53.0	58.9	143.7	▲	33.5	44.2	43.0	41.5	41.3	23.2	●

TABLE A1
Prevalence of undernourishment and progress towards the World Food Summit (WFS)[1] and the Millennium Development Goal (MDG)[2] targets in developing regions

Regions/subregions/countries	Number of people undernourished							Proportion of undernourished in total population						
	1990–92	2000–02	2005–07	2010–12	2014–16[3]	Change so far[4]	Progress towards WFS target[5]	1990–92	2000–02	2005–07	2010–12	2014–16[3]	Change so far[4]	Progress towards MDG target[5]
			(millions)			(%)				(%)				
Angola	6.8	7.0	5.4	3.8	3.2	−52.1	✳	63.5	48.9	31.3	18.9	14.2	−77.6	🟢
Cameroon	4.7	5.0	3.9	2.5	2.3	−50.5	✳	37.8	30.8	21.0	11.9	9.9	−73.7	🟢
Central African Republic	1.4	1.6	1.6	1.5	2.3	62.7	▲	47.3	42.9	40.6	33.7	47.7	1.0	🔴
Chad	3.6	3.5	4.1	4.8	4.7	28.8	▲	59.1	40.1	39.7	40.1	34.4	−41.9	⚪
Congo	1.1	1.0	1.2	1.3	1.4	34.5	▲	43.2	32.0	32.8	29.9	30.5	−29.6	🟡
Gabon	0.1	ns	ns	ns	ns	<−50.0	✳	11.7	<5.0	<5.0	<5.0	<5.0	na	🟢
Sao Tome and Principe	<0.1	<0.1	<0.1	<0.1	<0.1	−51.4	✳	22.9	17.6	8.9	5.9	6.6	−71.2	🟢
Southern Africa	**3.1**	**3.7**	**3.5**	**3.6**	**3.2**	**2.3**	▲	**7.2**	**7.1**	**6.2**	**6.1**	**5.2**	**−28.0**	⚪
Botswana	0.4	0.6	0.6	0.6	0.5	38.3	▲	25.1	36.0	32.2	28.7	24.1	−4.1	🟡
Lesotho	0.3	0.2	0.2	0.2	0.2	−6.3	◀▶	15.6	12.3	10.8	11.2	11.2	−28.0	🟡
Namibia	0.5	0.5	0.5	0.9	1.0	92.5	▲	35.9	27.3	26.0	39.4	42.3	18.0	🔴
South Africa	ns	ns	ns	ns	ns	>−50.0	▼	<5.0	<5.0	<5.0	<5.0	<5.0	na	🟢
Swaziland	0.1	0.2	0.2	0.3	0.3	144.4	▲	15.9	19.2	17.4	24.4	26.8	68.6	🔴
Western Africa	**44.6**	**35.9**	**32.3**	**30.4**	**33.7**	**−24.5**	◀▶	**24.2**	**15.0**	**11.8**	**9.7**	**9.6**	**−60.2**	🟢
Benin	1.5	1.6	1.3	1.2	0.8	−44.3	◀▶	28.1	22.4	15.0	11.9	7.5	−73.4	🟢
Burkina Faso	2.4	3.3	3.5	3.5	3.7	57.9	▲	26.0	27.6	25.5	21.7	20.7	−20.3	🟡
Cabo Verde	<0.1	<0.1	<0.1	<0.1	<0.1	−17.5	◀▶	16.1	19.2	14.4	12.1	9.4	−41.5	⚪
Côte d'Ivoire	1.3	2.7	2.5	2.8	2.8	111.8	▲	10.7	16.3	14.1	14.5	13.3	24.7	🔴
Gambia	0.1	0.2	0.2	0.1	0.1	−17.7	◀▶	13.3	13.0	14.9	7.1	5.3	−60.3	🟢
Ghana	7.1	3.1	2.3	1.4	ns	<−50.0	✳	47.3	15.9	10.5	5.6	<5.0	na	🟢
Guinea	1.5	2.3	2.2	2.0	2.0	37.5	▲	23.2	26.1	22.0	17.8	16.4	−29.0	🟡
Guinea-Bissau	0.2	0.3	0.4	0.4	0.4	53.6	▲	23.1	26.6	25.7	22.4	20.7	−10.5	🟡
Liberia	0.6	1.1	1.3	1.4	1.4	139.6	▲	29.0	37.8	38.8	34.7	31.9	10.0	🔴
Mali	1.4	1.3	1.1	ns	ns	<−50.0	✳	16.7	12.6	9.0	<5.0	<5.0	na	🟢
Mauritania	0.3	0.3	0.4	0.3	0.2	−24.7	◀▶	14.6	11.2	11.1	7.6	5.6	−61.6	🟢
Niger	2.2	2.3	2.0	1.7	1.8	−18.0	◀▶	27.7	20.5	14.5	10.5	9.5	−65.9	🟢
Nigeria	20.8	11.2	9.3	10.2	12.9	−38.1	◀▶	21.3	8.9	6.5	6.2	7.0	−67.0	🟢
Senegal	1.9	2.9	2.4	1.9	3.7	93.1	▲	24.5	28.2	21.1	14.3	24.6	0.1	🔴
Sierra Leone	1.7	1.7	2.0	1.6	1.4	−18.6	◀▶	42.8	40.2	37.1	27.0	22.3	−47.9	⚪
Togo	1.5	1.4	1.4	1.2	0.8	−44.6	▼	37.9	28.7	24.2	18.9	11.4	−69.9	🟢
ASIA	**741.9**	**636.5**	**665.5**	**546.9**	**511.7**	**−31.0**	◀▶	**23.6**	**17.6**	**17.3**	**13.5**	**12.1**	**−48.9**	🟢
Caucasus and Central Asia	**9.6**	**10.9**	**8.4**	**7.1**	**5.8**	**−39.9**	◀▶	**14.1**	**15.3**	**11.3**	**8.9**	**7.0**	**−50.8**	🟢
Armenia	0.9	0.7	0.2	0.2	0.2	−80.8	✳	27.3	23.0	8.2	6.8	5.8	−78.8	🟢
Azerbaijan	1.8	1.4	ns	ns	ns	<−50.0	✳	23.6	17.1	<5.0	<5.0	<5.0	na	🟢
Georgia	3.0	0.8	0.3	0.4	0.3	−89.4	✳	56.5	16.3	6.0	10.1	7.4	−86.8	🟢
Kazakhstan	ns	ns	0.8	ns	ns	>−50.0	◀▶	<5.0	<5.0	5.0	<5.0	<5.0	na	🟢
Kyrgyzstan	0.7	0.8	0.5	0.4	0.3	−53.1	✳	15.9	16.7	9.4	7.2	6.0	−62.6	🟢
Tajikistan	1.6	2.5	2.8	2.9	2.9	78.3	▲	28.1	39.5	40.5	36.8	33.2	18.2	🔴

TABLE A1
Prevalence of undernourishment and progress towards the World Food Summit (WFS)[1] and the Millennium Development Goal (MDG)[2] targets in developing regions

Regions/subregions/countries	Number of people undernourished (millions)					Change so far[4] (%)	Progress towards WFS target[5]	Proportion of undernourished in total population (%)					Change so far[4]	Progress towards MDG target[5]
	1990–92	2000–02	2005–07	2010–12	2014–16[3]			1990–92	2000–02	2005–07	2010–12	2014–16[3]		
Turkmenistan	0.4	0.4	0.2	ns	ns	<−50.0	✳	8.6	8.4	5.1	<5.0	<5.0	na	●
Uzbekistan	ns	3.6	3.3	2.2	ns	>0.0	▲	<5.0	14.4	12.4	7.7	<5.0	na	●
Eastern Asia	**295.4**	**221.7**	**217.6**	**174.7**	**145.1**	**−50.9**	✳	**23.2**	**16.0**	**15.2**	**11.8**	**9.6**	**−58.5**	●
Eastern Asia (excluding China)	**6.4**	**10.4**	**10.3**	**11.5**	**11.3**	**77.6**	▲	**9.6**	**14.6**	**13.9**	**15.1**	**14.6**	**50.9**	●
China	289.0	211.2	207.3	163.2	133.8	−53.7	✳	23.9	16.0	15.3	11.7	9.3	−60.9	●
Democratic People's Republic of Korea	4.8	8.7	8.5	10.3	10.5	118.5	▲	23.3	37.7	35.5	42.0	41.6	78.4	●
Mongolia	0.7	0.9	0.9	0.7	0.6	−9.8	◀▶	29.9	36.1	34.0	24.5	20.5	−31.5	●
Republic of Korea	ns	ns	ns	ns	ns	<−50.0	✳	<5.0	<5.0	<5.0	<5.0	<5.0	na	●
Southern Asia	**291.2**	**272.3**	**319.1**	**274.2**	**281.4**	**−3.4**	◀▶	**23.9**	**18.5**	**20.1**	**16.1**	**15.7**	**−34.4**	●
Southern Asia (excluding India)	**81.1**	**86.7**	**85.3**	**84.3**	**86.8**	**7.0**	▲	**24.5**	**21.0**	**19.0**	**17.5**	**17.0**	**−30.6**	●
Afghanistan	3.8	10.0	8.3	7.1	8.6	126.1	▲	29.5	46.7	32.3	24.3	26.8	−9.0	●
Bangladesh	36.0	27.7	24.3	26.5	26.3	−27.0	◀▶	32.8	20.6	16.8	17.3	16.4	−49.9	●
India	210.1	185.5	233.8	189.9	194.6	−7.4	◀▶	23.7	17.5	20.5	15.6	15.2	−36.0	●
Iran (Islamic Republic of)	2.9	3.8	4.7	4.7	ns	>0.0	▲	5.1	5.6	6.6	6.2	<5.0	na	●
Maldives	<0.1	<0.1	<0.1	<0.1	<0.1	−31.6	▼	12.2	11.9	15.4	8.7	5.2	−57.6	●
Nepal	4.2	5.2	4.1	2.5	2.2	−47.3	◀▶	22.8	21.9	15.8	9.2	7.8	−65.6	●
Pakistan	28.7	34.4	38.1	38.3	41.4	44.2	▲	25.1	23.4	23.7	21.8	22.0	−12.4	●
Sri Lanka	5.4	5.7	5.9	5.3	4.7	−11.6	◀▶	30.6	29.7	29.1	25.3	22.0	−28.3	●
South-Eastern Asia	**137.5**	**117.6**	**103.2**	**72.5**	**60.5**	**−56.0**	✳	**30.6**	**22.3**	**18.3**	**12.1**	**9.6**	**−68.5**	●
Brunei Darussalam	ns	ns	ns	ns	ns	>−50.0	◀▶	<5.0	<5.0	<5.0	<5.0	<5.0	na	●
Cambodia	3.0	3.6	2.7	2.5	2.2	−26.1	◀▶	32.1	28.5	19.6	16.8	14.2	−55.8	●
Indonesia	35.9	38.3	42.7	26.9	19.4	−45.9	▼	19.7	18.1	18.8	11.1	7.6	−61.6	●
Lao People's Democratic Republic	1.9	2.1	1.6	1.4	1.3	−30.6	◀▶	42.8	37.9	26.9	21.4	18.5	−56.8	●
Malaysia	1.0	ns	ns	ns	ns	>−50.0	◀▶	5.1	<5.0	<5.0	<5.0	<5.0	na	●
Myanmar	26.8	24.3	17.0	9.4	7.7	−71.4	✳	62.6	49.6	33.7	18.0	14.2	−77.4	●
Philippines	16.7	16.1	14.3	12.7	13.7	−17.9	◀▶	26.3	20.3	16.4	13.4	13.5	−48.8	●
Thailand	19.8	11.6	7.7	6.0	5.0	−74.9	✳	34.6	18.4	11.7	8.9	7.4	−78.7	●
Timor-Leste	0.4	0.4	0.3	0.3	0.3	−10.0	◀▶	45.2	41.6	34.0	31.2	26.9	−40.4	●
Viet Nam	32.1	20.7	15.9	12.2	10.3	−68.0	✳	45.6	25.4	18.5	13.6	11.0	−75.8	●
Western Asia[20]	**8.2**	**14.0**	**17.2**	**18.4**	**18.9**	**129.5**	▲	**6.4**	**8.6**	**9.3**	**8.8**	**8.4**	**32.2**	●
Iraq	1.4	5.8	7.3	7.8	8.1	470.4	▲	7.9	23.5	26.0	24.5	22.8	189.7	●
Jordan	0.2	0.3	ns	ns	ns	>−50.0	◀▶	5.5	6.0	<5.0	<5.0	<5.0	na	●
Kuwait	0.8	ns	ns	ns	ns	<−50.0	✳	39.4	<5.0	<5.0	<5.0	<5.0	na	●
Lebanon	ns	ns	ns	ns	ns	>0.0	▲	<5.0	<5.0	<5.0	<5.0	<5.0	na	●
Oman	0.3	0.2	0.2	ns	ns	<−50.0	✳	15.1	9.3	7.9	<5.0	<5.0	na	●
Saudi Arabia	ns	ns	ns	ns	ns	>−50.0	◀▶	<5.0	<5.0	<5.0	<5.0	<5.0	na	●
Turkey	ns	ns	ns	ns	ns	<−50.0	✳	<5.0	<5.0	<5.0	<5.0	<5.0	na	●
United Arab Emirates	ns	ns	ns	ns	ns	>0.0	▲	<5.0	<5.0	<5.0	<5.0	<5.0	na	●
Yemen	3.6	5.3	6.1	6.1	6.7	85.6	▲	28.9	29.4	29.7	26.3	26.1	−9.7	●

TABLE A1
Prevalence of undernourishment and progress towards the World Food Summit (WFS)[1] and the Millennium Development Goal (MDG)[2] targets in developing regions

Regions/subregions/countries	Number of people undernourished (millions)					Change so far[4] (%)	Progress towards WFS target[5]	Proportion of undernourished in total population (%)					Change so far[4]	Progress towards MDG target[5]
	1990–92	2000–02	2005–07	2010–12	2014–16[3]			1990–92	2000–02	2005–07	2010–12	2014–16[3]		
LATIN AMERICA AND THE CARIBBEAN	66.1	60.4	47.1	38.3	34.3	–48.0	✳	14.7	11.4	8.4	6.4	5.5	–62.7	🟢
Caribbean[21]	8.1	8.2	8.3	7.3	7.5	–7.2	◀▶	27.0	24.4	23.5	19.8	19.8	–26.6	🟡
Barbados	ns	<0.1	<0.1	ns	ns	>0.0	▲	<5.0	5.2	6.7	<5.0	<5.0	na	🟢
Cuba	0.6	ns	ns	ns	ns	<–50.0	✳	5.7	<5.0	<5.0	<5.0	<5.0	na	🟢
Dominican Republic	2.5	2.5	2.3	1.6	1.3	–48.5	✳	34.3	28.4	24.2	15.9	12.3	–64.3	🟢
Haiti	4.4	4.8	5.4	4.9	5.7	27.7	▲	61.1	55.2	57.1	49.3	53.4	–12.6	🟡
Jamaica	0.2	0.2	0.2	0.2	0.2	–8.3	◀▶	10.4	7.3	7.0	8.3	8.1	–22.3	⚪
Saint Vincent and the Grenadines	<0.1	<0.1	<0.1	<0.1	<0.1	–69.7	✳	20.7	16.8	9.2	6.4	6.2	–70.1	🟢
Trinidad and Tobago	0.2	0.2	0.2	0.1	0.1	–35.4	▼	12.6	11.9	11.7	9.9	7.4	–41.0	⚪
Latin America	58.0	52.1	38.8	31.0	26.8	–53.8	✳	13.9	10.5	7.3	5.5	<5.0	na	🟢
Central America	12.6	11.8	11.6	11.3	11.4	–9.6	◀▶	10.7	8.3	7.6	6.9	6.6	–38.2	🟡
Belize	<0.1	<0.1	ns	<0.1	<0.1	16.1	▲	9.7	5.8	<5.0	5.7	6.2	–36.2	🟡
Costa Rica	0.2	0.2	0.2	0.3	ns	>0.0	▲	5.2	5.1	5.6	5.3	<5.0	na	🟢
El Salvador	0.9	0.6	0.7	0.8	0.8	–9.8	◀▶	16.2	10.6	10.7	12.6	12.4	–23.8	🟡
Guatemala	1.4	2.3	2.1	2.2	2.5	86.9	▲	14.9	20.4	15.9	14.8	15.6	4.7	🟠
Honduras	1.2	1.2	1.2	1.1	1.0	–11.5	◀▶	23.0	18.5	16.4	14.6	12.2	–47.1	⚪
Mexico	6.0	ns	ns	ns	ns	>–50.0	◀▶	6.9	<5.0	<5.0	<5.0	<5.0	na	🟢
Nicaragua	2.3	1.6	1.3	1.2	1.0	–55.0	✳	54.4	31.3	23.2	19.5	16.6	–69.5	🟢
Panama	0.7	0.9	0.8	0.5	0.4	–43.8	▼	26.4	27.6	22.9	13.4	9.5	–64.2	🟢
South America	45.4	40.3	27.2	ns	ns	<–50.0	✳	15.1	11.4	7.2	<5.0	<5.0	na	🟢
Argentina	ns	ns	ns	ns	ns	<–50.0	✳	<5.0	<5.0	<5.0	<5.0	<5.0	na	🟢
Bolivia (Plurinational State of)	2.6	2.8	2.8	2.5	1.8	–33.6	◀▶	38.0	32.8	29.9	24.5	15.9	–58.1	🟢
Brazil	22.6	19.9	ns	ns	ns	<–50.0	✳	14.8	11.2	<5.0	<5.0	<5.0	na	🟢
Chile	1.2	ns	ns	ns	ns	<–50.0	✳	9.0	<5.0	<5.0	<5.0	<5.0	na	🟢
Colombia	5.0	3.9	4.2	5.3	4.4	–12.1	◀▶	14.6	9.6	9.7	11.2	8.8	–39.8	⚪
Ecuador	2.0	2.4	2.6	2.0	1.8	–12.3	◀▶	19.4	18.6	18.8	12.8	10.9	–44.0	⚪
Guyana	0.2	<0.1	<0.1	<0.1	<0.1	–48.2	✳	22.8	9.7	10.4	11.8	10.6	–53.6	🟢
Paraguay	0.9	0.7	0.7	0.8	0.7	–14.0	◀▶	19.5	12.9	11.2	12.1	10.4	–46.6	⚪
Peru	7.0	5.4	5.3	3.2	2.3	–66.6	✳	31.6	20.7	18.9	10.7	7.5	–76.2	🟢
Suriname	<0.1	<0.1	<0.1	<0.1	<0.1	–31.2	◀▶	15.5	13.9	11.5	8.3	8.0	–48.2	🟢
Uruguay	0.3	ns	ns	ns	ns	<–50.0	✳	8.6	<5.0	<5.0	<5.0	<5.0	na	🟢
Venezuela (Bolivarian Republic of)	2.8	3.8	2.5	ns	ns	<–50.0	✳	14.1	15.3	9.0	<5.0	<5.0	na	🟢
OCEANIA[22]	1.0	1.3	1.3	1.3	1.4	51.5	▲	15.7	16.5	15.4	13.5	14.2	–9.9	🟡
Fiji	<0.1	ns	ns	ns	ns	>–50.0	◀▶	6.6	<5.0	<5.0	<5.0	<5.0	na	🟢
Kiribati	<0.1	ns	ns	ns	ns	>–50.0	◀▶	7.5	<5.0	<5.0	<5.0	<5.0	na	🟢
Samoa	<0.1	<0.1	ns	ns	ns	<–50.0	✳	10.7	5.2	<5.0	<5.0	<5.0	na	🟢
Solomon Islands	<0.1	<0.1	<0.1	<0.1	<0.1	–17.1	◀▶	24.8	15.0	12.0	10.7	11.3	–54.5	🟢
Vanuatu	<0.1	<0.1	<0.1	<0.1	<0.1	0.1	▲	11.2	8.2	7.0	6.1	6.4	–42.8	🟡

Methodology for assessing food security and progress towards the international hunger targets

Suite of food security indicators

Food security is a complex phenomenon, manifested in numerous physical conditions with multiple causes. *The State of Food Insecurity in the World 2013* introduced a suite of food security indicators, which measures separately the four dimensions of food security to allow a more nuanced assessment of food insecurity.

Updated data for the suite of food security indicators can be viewed and downloaded from FAOSTAT (at http://faostat3.fao.org/download/D/FS/E) and the FAO website (at http://www.fao.org/economic/ess/ess-fs/ess-fadata/en/).

FIGURE **A2.1**

Suite of food security indicators

FOOD SECURITY INDICATORS	DIMENSION
Average dietary energy supply adequacy Average value of food production	AVAILABILITY
Share of dietary energy supply derived from cereals, roots and tubers Average protein supply Average supply of protein of animal origin	
Percentage of paved roads over total roads Road density Rail lines density	ACCESS
Gross domestic product (in purchasing power parity)	
Domestic food price index	
Prevalence of undernourishment Share of food expenditure of the poor Depth of the food deficit Prevalence of food inadequacy	
Cereal import dependency ratio Percent of arable land equipped for irrigation Value of food imports over total merchandise exports	STABILITY
Political stability and absence of violence/terrorism Domestic food price volatility Per capita food production variability Per capita food supply variability	
Access to improved water sources Access to improved sanitation facilities	UTILIZATION
Percentage of children under 5 years of age affected by wasting Percentage of children under 5 years of age who are stunted Percentage of children under 5 years of age who are underweight Percentage of adults who are underweight Prevalence of anaemia among pregnant women Prevalence of anaemia among children under 5 years of age Prevalence of vitamin A deficiency in the population Prevalence of iodine deficiency in the population	

Source: FAO.

Prevalence of undernourishment indicator

The FAO prevalence of undernourishment (PoU) indicator measures the probability that a randomly selected individual from the reference population is found to consume less than his/her calorie requirement for an active and healthy life. It is written as:

$$PoU \equiv \int_{x < MDER} f(x)\, dx$$

where $f(x)$ is the probability density function of per capita calorie consumption. The probability distribution used to infer the habitual levels of dietary energy consumption in a population, $f(x)$, refers to a typical level of daily energy consumption during a year. The probability distribution $f(x)$ and the minimum dietary energy requirement (MDER) are associated with a representative individual of the population, of average age, sex, stature and physical activity level.

Estimating the PoU requires the identification of a functional form for $f(x)$, chosen from a parametric family. The parameters that characterize $f(x)$ are the mean level of per capita dietary energy consumption (DEC) in calories; the MDER; the coefficient of variation (CV) as a parameter accounting for inequality in food consumption; and a skewness (SK) parameter accounting for asymmetry in the distribution.

To implement this methodology it is necessary to: (i) choose a functional form for the distribution of food consumption $f(x)$; (ii) identify values for the three parameters, that is, for mean food consumption (DEC), its variability (CV) and its asymmetry (SK); and (iii) compute the MDER threshold.

The choice of a functional form for the distribution

Starting from the Sixth World Food Survey in 1996,[67] the distribution was assumed to be lognormal. This model is convenient for analytical purposes, but has limited flexibility, especially in capturing the skewness of the distribution.

As part of the revisions made for the 2012 edition of *The State of Food Insecurity in the World*, the methodology moved away from the exclusive use of the two-parameter lognormal distribution to adopt the more flexible three-parameter skew-normal and skew-lognormal families.[68] The flexibility gained from the additional parameter allows for independent characterization of the asymmetry of the distribution.

As a further refinement, the data themselves are used in this report to inform the decision regarding the appropriate distributional form.[69] In this way, the empirical skewness from the distribution of per capita calorie consumption derived from national household surveys (NHS)[70] is applied as a selection criterion. Using the skewness implied by the lognormal as an upper limit for the level of asymmetry, the skew-lognormal, which embeds the lognormal as a special case, is used as an intermediate step to the skew-normal distribution, which itself is a more general form of the normal distribution. The resulting model makes it possible to account for reductions in inequality of food consumption, such as those made by targeted food intervention programmes, ensuring a smooth transition towards a distribution in which food consumption is symmetric.

Estimating and projecting mean food consumption

To compute per capita DEC in a country, FAO has traditionally relied on food balance sheets, which are available for more than 180 countries. In most countries, this choice was due mainly to the lack of suitable surveys conducted regularly. Through data on production, trade and utilization of food commodities, the total amount of dietary energy available for human consumption in a country for a one-year period is derived using food composition data, allowing computation of an estimate of per capita dietary energy supply.

During the revision for *The State of Food Insecurity in the World 2012*, a parameter that captures food losses during distribution at the retail level was introduced in an attempt to obtain more accurate values of per capita consumption. Region-specific calorie losses were estimated from data provided in a recent FAO study[71] and ranged from 2 percent of the quantity distributed for dry grains, to 10 percent for perishable products, such as fresh fruits and vegetables.

The last period for which the PoU is estimated is the three-year average 2014–16. This choice arises from the need to maintain consistency with previous assessments of undernourishment – which were based on three-year averages since 1990–92 – and the monitoring of the Millennium Development Goals and the World Food Summit goal, which ends in 2015 (see next section). The last period has to be a three-year average centred on year 2015, that is, 2014–16. Therefore, per capita DEC needs to be computed and projected up to the year 2016.

The latest available data from food balance sheets refer to year 2013 for most countries,[72] while for other countries data are available only until 2011. Therefore, additional sources were needed to estimate the DEC for the subsequent years. The main source of missing data for 2012, 2013 and 2014 are the food consumption estimates from the short-term market outlook prepared by the Trade and Markets Division (EST) of FAO. The Division computes per capita availability of major commodities – cereals, meats, oilseeds and sugar – for most countries of the world. These estimates were used to pro-rate the food balance sheet data to arrive at forecasts for 2012, 2013 and 2014. These forecasts are updated every six months, and need to be supplemented by projections for the most recent years.

The Holt-Winters distributed lag model was used to project the DEC for 2015 and 2016; in some cases, this model was also applied to compute projections for 2014, when EST data were not available or unreliable. The Holt-Winters model uses a process known as exponential smoothing, which attributes higher weights to more recent data and progressively less weight to older observations. Weights decrease in each period by a constant amount, which lies on an exponential curve. Where the Holt-Winters distributed lag model did not produce plausible results, simpler forecasting methods were used, such as linear or exponential trend extrapolations. For some countries, particularly where EST estimates appeared to provide implausible results, the econometric forecasting had to be applied for the whole projection period.

Annex 2

Estimating coefficients of variation and skewness[73]

A new data treatment method

Variability (CV) and skewness (SK) parameters are derived from NHS wherever they are available and reliable. These surveys typically collect information on food as part of the expenditure module. Data from these surveys, when taken as observations of individual habitual consumption, are affected by high variability. It is therefore essential to apply data treatment methods before parameters are estimated. This is especially the case for the SK parameter, which is sensitive to the presence of extreme values.[74]

The method applied in this edition of *The State of Food Insecurity in the World* to assess the robustness of statistics for a sample is known as the "leave-out-one cross-validation" approach. With this approach, for a sample of size *n*, subsamples of size (*n* − 1) are created in which each observation is systematically left out of one subsample. For each subsample, the sensitivity of the statistic of interest – in this case, the SK parameter – to the excluded observation can be analysed, and observations that have a large impact are removed. The method allows a robust calculation of the SK parameter that is insensitive to any single observation found in the dataset.

Controlling for excess variability

As the original purpose of NHS is to measure the levels and changes in living conditions of the population, the data collected typically pertain to food acquisition over a given reference period. However, the aim of the food security analyses in this report is to capture habitual food consumption, which is expected to be less variable than food acquisition. Therefore, excess variability is controlled by assuming a stable relationship between income and consumption in calories, which nets out excess variability caused by some households boosting their food stocks while other households deplete theirs. In the past, this control for excess variability has been accomplished by grouping household food consumption levels according to income deciles.[75]

In this edition of *The State of Food Insecurity in the World*, an extension of the method described above is used, based on a linear regression linking the log of per capita income to per capita calorie consumption, along with indicator variables for the month in which the survey was conducted, to control for seasonality. The regression can be written as:

$$PPC_i = \beta_0 + \beta_1 * \log(inc_i) + \beta_2 Month_{1,i} + \beta_3 Month_{2,i} + \cdots + \beta_m Month_{m-1,i}$$

where PPC_i is the per capita calorie consumption for household *i*, β_0 is an intercept term, β_1 is a regression parameter defining the linear relationship between the log of income and food consumption, and $Month_{j,i}$ is an indicator variable with value 1 if the survey for household *i* took place in month *j*. The variability in food consumption due to income is then calculated from the fitted values of the regression adjusted for seasonality.

A new estimation of indirect CVs

The procedure described so far is used in countries where one or more reliable NHS are available. Where this is not the case, so-called indirect estimates for the variability in food consumption are used. Indirect CVs were estimated by using the relationships between the CVs obtained from available household survey data and some key macroeconomic variables. In the past, the PoU indicator methodology was frequently criticized for holding CVs – which account for inequality in food consumption – constant over time for most countries.[76] This practice does not take into account economic progress within a country and changes in the distribution of food consumption. To address this issue, in this report, indirect estimates have been updated from the year 2000 onwards by using a revised relationship among the CVs due to income and macroeconomic variables that also takes into account changes in food prices.

To fully investigate the effects of food price changes on food access, measures of national prices should be used. In collaboration with the World Bank, FAO has developed a relative price of food indicator using data from the International Comparison Program[77] and consumer food price indices available on FAOSTAT.[78] The indicator is designed to capture changes in domestic food prices that are comparable over time and among countries. The ratio of food and general consumption in purchasing power parity (PPP) terms is projected forwards and backwards in time using the ratio of the country's consumer food price index to the country's general consumer price index, relative to that of the United States of America.

Using the most comprehensive dataset of Gini coefficients available,[79] a regression has been used to relate the variability in food consumption due to income to the log of GDP, the Gini coefficient, and the log of the relative price of food indicator. The GDP and relative price of food indicators are included on the log-scale, implying that changes in these variables at low values will have a larger impact on the CV due to income. To ensure cross-country comparability at different points in time, per capita GDP in constant 2005 international dollars in PPP terms, calculated by the World Bank, has been used. Regional indicators have been included for Africa, the Americas, Asia, and Western Asia. An interaction term between the GDP and the relative food price indicator has been included to allow for differential effects of the price of food at different levels of GDP. As there are multiple observations – more than one survey – for some countries, a weighted regression was used in which each observation is weighted by one over the number of surveys for that country.

With the parameters from the regression described above, the variability in food consumption due to income has been updated for countries with available Gini coefficients and available data on the relative price of food and GDP. Note that the Gini coefficients in the World Bank database differ in terms of whether they are calculated with reference to the household or the individual, consumption or expenditure, and gross or net income – these differences can make comparability across different types of Gini coefficient difficult.[80] For this reason, care was taken to ensure that the same type of Gini calculation was used within a single country and, to maintain cross-country comparability, only relative changes in the predicted values from the regression were used to update the CV parameter. The resulting updates take into account economic progress in a country as well as changes in relative food prices, allowing for a more complete picture of inequality in food consumption.

A new computation of variability due to requirement

To obtain the total variability in food consumption used to calculate the PoU, the variability that is due to income ($CV|y$) is added to the variability due to all other factors that are not correlated with income ($CV|r$):

$$CV(x) = \sqrt{(CV|y)^2 + (CV|r)^2}$$

Much of the variability orthogonal to income is due to differences in energy requirement, which are in turn largely determined by population structure as well as by physical activity levels, lifestyles, access to safe drinking-water, and progress in health care and disease reduction. Previous analyses showed small variability in this subcomponent across countries and over time, compared with the income component, and the variability due to requirement has been maintained at a fixed value.

To take into account the world's rapidly changing population structure,[81] time-varying country estimates for the variability in food consumption due to requirement have been calculated. Using estimates for the average dietary energy requirement by sex and age class[82] and corresponding population ratios[83] as weights, the variance due to requirement is estimated for a given country in a given year. Further work is under way to capture the rest of the variability that is orthogonal to income. The revision discussed here allows estimates of the variability in food consumption to reflect more accurately demographic differences across countries and demographic evolution within a country.

Estimating the MDER threshold

To calculate the MDER threshold, FAO uses normative energy requirement standards from a joint FAO/WHO/United Nations University expert consultation in 2001. These standards are obtained by calculating the needs for basic metabolism – that is, the energy expended by the human body in a state of rest – and multiplying them by a factor that takes into account physical activity, referred to as the physical activity level (PAL) index.

As individual metabolic efficiency and physical activity levels vary within population groups of the same age and sex, energy requirements are expressed as ranges for such groups. To derive the MDER threshold, the minimum of each range for adults and adolescents is specified on the basis of the distribution of ideal body weights and the mid-point of the values of the physical activity level (PAL) index associated with a sedentary lifestyle (1.55). The lowest body weight for a given height that is compatible with good health is estimated from the fifth percentile of the distribution of body mass indices in healthy populations.

Once the minimum requirement for each sex-age group has been established, the population-level MDER threshold is obtained as a weighted average, considering the relative frequency of individuals in each group as weights. The threshold is determined with reference to light physical activity, normally associated with a sedentary lifestyle. However, this does not negate the fact that the population also includes individuals engaged in moderate and intense physical activity. It is just one way of avoiding the overestimation of food inadequacy when only food consumption levels are observed that cannot be individually matched to the varying requirements.

A frequent misconception when assessing food inadequacy based on observed food consumption data is to refer to the mid-point in the overall range of requirements as a threshold for identifying inadequate energy consumption in the population. This would lead to significantly biased estimates: even in groups composed of only well-nourished people, roughly half of these individuals will have intake levels below mean requirements, as the group will include people engaged in low physical activity. Using the mean requirement as a threshold would certainly produce an overestimate, as all adequately nourished individuals with less than average requirements would be misclassified as undernourished.[84]

MDER thresholds are updated every two years based on regular revisions of the population assessments of the United Nations Population Division and data on population heights from various sources, most notably the Monitoring and Evaluation to Assess and Use Results of Demographic and Health Surveys project coordinated by the United States Agency for International Development (USAID). This edition of *The State of Food Insecurity in the World* uses updated population estimates from the 2012 revision published by the United Nations Population Division in June 2013. When data on population heights are not available, reference is made either to data on heights from countries where similar ethnicities prevail, or to models that use partial information to estimate heights for various sex and age classes.

Limitations of the methodology and frequent critiques

The FAO methodology for estimating undernourishment has been subject to long-standing and wide debate. The methodology suffers from several limitations, which need to be acknowledged and taken into account when analysing the results presented in this report.

First, the indicator is based on a narrow definition of hunger, covering only chronically inadequate dietary energy intake lasting for over one year. Energy intake is a very specific aspect of food insecurity, which applies where conditions are more severe. Individuals experiencing difficulties in obtaining enough food are likely to switch towards cheaper sources of energy and to compromise the quality of their food intake in a way that can create substantial damage.[85] To address this limitation, the FAO suite of food security indicators has been presented since the 2013 edition of *The State of Food Insecurity in the World*. The suite comprises indicators that reflect a broader concept of food insecurity and hunger and allows consideration of their multifaceted nature.

Second, the PoU indicator cannot capture within-year fluctuations in the capacity to acquire enough energy from food, which may themselves be causes of significant stresses for the population. Within-year fluctuations can also affect the quality of the diet, as consumers will resort to cheaper foods during periods when access becomes more difficult.

Third, the FAO methodology for computing undernourishment cannot take into account any bias that may exist in intra-household distribution of foods,[86] such as that arising from cultural habits or gender-based habits and beliefs. As seen, the parameters that describe the distribution of food across the population are derived from household-level surveys, rather than from information that refers to individuals.

A final and significant limitation of the FAO methodology for computing the prevalence of undernourishment is that it does not provide information on the degree of severity of the food insecurity conditions experienced by a population. The parametric model described in this annex only allows for estimates of the undernourished share in a population, but is silent about the composition of undernourishment within that part of the population.

In the debate on measuring undernourishment, the FAO methodology has attracted two frequent criticisms:

- The indicator underestimates undernourishment, as it assumes a level of physical activity associated with a sedentary lifestyle, while poor people are often engaged in physically demanding activities.
- The methodology is based on macrodata, whereas microdata from surveys allow accurate measurement of food consumption.

On the first criticism, ideally, undernourishment should be assessed at the individual level by comparing individual energy requirements with individual energy intakes. This would enable the classification of each person in the population as undernourished or not. However, this approach is not feasible for two reasons: individual energy requirements are practically unobservable with standard data collection methods; and individual food consumption is currently measured with precision in only a few countries and for relatively limited samples. The individual-level consumption data that can be estimated from NHS are largely approximated owing to disparities in intra-household food allocation, the variability of individual energy requirements, and the day-to-day variability of food consumption that can arise for reasons independent of food insecurity. The solution adopted by FAO has been to estimate the PoU with reference to the population as a whole, summarized through a representative individual, and to combine available microdata on food consumption with macrodata. Within the population, there is a range of values for energy requirements that are compatible with healthy status, given that body weight, metabolic efficiency and physical activity levels vary. It follows that only values below the minimum of such a range can be associated with undernourishment, in a probabilistic sense. Hence, for the PoU to indicate that a randomly selected individual in a population is undernourished, the appropriate threshold is the lower end of the range of energy requirements.

As for the second criticism, the FAO methodology in fact combines available microdata on food consumption derived from surveys with macrodata from food balance sheets. Food balance sheets provide information on the amount of food that is available for consumption after taking into account all possible alternative uses of the food items; hence, they provide approximate measures of per capita consumption, which are available for a large number of countries and are comparable. The methodology adopted for computing these data is currently under revision, together with the estimates of waste parameters used to derive the DEC, so the level of accuracy is expected to increase in the next few years. Survey data, where available and reliable, are used in the FAO methodology to compute the variability (CV) and skewness (SK) parameters that characterize the distribution of food consumption $f(x)$. It is therefore essential that household surveys collecting food consumption data are improved to obtain more accurate measures of undernourishment. Such improvements will require both promoting greater standardization across NHS, and conducting more refined surveys that capture food intake at the individual level. At the moment, few surveys accurately capture habitual food consumption at the individual level and collect sufficient information on the anthropometric characteristics and activity levels of each surveyed individual; in other words, very few surveys would allow for an estimation of the relevant energy requirement threshold at the individual level.

To conclude, the quality of the PoU estimates depends heavily on the quality of the background data used in the estimation. Hence, to obtain better estimates of undernourishment it is important to improve food consumption data through the design and implementation of high-quality nationally representative surveys that are comparable over time and across countries.

Criteria for identifying countries that have reached the MDG 1c hunger target and the 1996 World Food Summit goal

Following the recommendation of the Committee on World Food Security (CFS),[87] countries that have reached the two targets have been identified on the basis of the number of undernourished and the PoU.

The 1996 World Food Summit goal was defined in the Rome Declaration on World Food Security,[88] in which the representatives of 182 governments pledged "... *to eradicate hunger in all countries, with an immediate view to reducing the number of undernourished people to half their present level no later than 2015.*" Estimates of the number of undernourished were used by FAO as a basis to monitor progress towards this goal.

With the establishment of the Millennium Development Goals, progress indicators were identified for each goal, to track progress at national and global levels. The reference period was identified as the 25 years between 1990 and 2015. The first MDG, or MDG 1, includes three distinct targets:

- halving global poverty;
- achieving full and productive employment and decent work for all; and
- halving the proportion of people who suffer from hunger by 2015.

The progress indicator for the third target, known as Target 1c, is the PoU.

FAO began monitoring progress towards the WFS and the MDG 1c hunger targets at the end of 1990s, using the three-year period 1990–92 as a starting point. Both targets are to be reached by the end of 2015. To maintain consistency with the initial time period and the definition of the targets of the MDGs, progress has been assessed up to a three-year average period centred on 2015, that is, 2014–16.

At the same time, achievement of all the MDGs is meant to be assessed for the 25-year period, from 1990 to 2015, but for the PoU, observations were only available for the 24-year period from 1990–92 and 2014–16. To address this potential inconsistency, the 50 percent reduction in the number of undernourished and the PoU needed to reach the WFS and the MDG 1c hunger targets, respectively, has been adjusted by a factor of 24/25. In practice, this means that a cut-off point of 48 percent has been used.

Glossary of selected terms used in the report

Anthropometry. Use of human body measurements to obtain information about nutritional status.

Body mass index (BMI). The ratio of weight-for-height measured as the weight in kilograms divided by the square of height in metres.

Dietary energy intake. The energy content of food consumed.

Dietary energy requirement (DER). The amount of dietary energy required by an individual to maintain body functions, health and normal activity.

Dietary energy supply (DES). Food available for human consumption, expressed in kilocalories per person per day (kcal/person/day). At country level, it is calculated as the food remaining for human use after deduction of all non-food utilizations (i.e. food = production + imports + stock withdrawals – exports – industrial use – animal feed – seed – wastage – additions to stock). Wastage includes losses of usable products occurring along distribution chains from farm gate (or port of import) up to the retail level.

Dietary energy supply adequacy. Dietary energy supply as a percentage of the average dietary energy requirement.

Food insecurity. A situation that exists when people lack secure access to sufficient amounts of safe and nutritious food for normal growth and development and an active and healthy life. It may be caused by the unavailability of food, insufficient purchasing power, inappropriate distribution or inadequate use of food at the household level. Food insecurity, poor conditions of health and sanitation and inappropriate care and feeding practices are the major causes of poor nutritional status. Food insecurity may be chronic, seasonal or transitory.

Food security. A situation that exists when all people, at all times, have physical, social and economic access to sufficient, safe and nutritious food that meets their dietary needs and food preferences for an active and healthy life. Based on this definition, four food security dimensions can be identified: food availability, economic and physical access to food, food utilization and stability over time.

Hunger. In this report the term hunger is used as being synonymous with chronic undernourishment.

Kilocalorie (kcal). A unit of measurement of energy. One kilocalorie equals 1 000 calories. In the International System of Units (SI), the universal unit of energy is the joule (J). One kilocalorie = 4.184 kilojoules (kJ).

Macronutrients. In this document, the proteins, carbohydrates and fats that are available to be used for energy. They are measured in grams.

Malnutrition. An abnormal physiological condition caused by inadequate, unbalanced or excessive consumption of macronutrients and/or micronutrients. Malnutrition includes undernutrition and overnutrition as well as micronutrient deficiencies.

Micronutrients. Vitamins, minerals and certain other substances that are required by the body in small amounts. They are measured in milligrams or micrograms.

Minimum dietary energy requirement (MDER). In a specified age/sex category, the minimum amount of dietary energy per person that is considered adequate to meet the energy needs at a minimum acceptable BMI of an individual engaged in low physical activity. If referring to an entire population, the minimum energy requirement is the weighted average of the minimum energy requirements of the different age/sex groups. It is expressed as kilocalories per person per day.

Nutrition security. A situation that exists when secure access to an appropriately nutritious diet is coupled with a sanitary environment, adequate health services and care, in order to ensure a healthy and active life for all household members. Nutrition security differs from food security in that it also considers the aspects of adequate caring practices, health and hygiene in addition to dietary adequacy.

Nutrition-sensitive intervention. Interventions designed to address the underlying determinants of nutrition (which include household food security, care for mothers and children and primary health care services and sanitation) but not necessarily having nutrition as the predominant goal.

Nutritional status. The physiological state of an individual that results from the relationship between nutrient intake and requirements and from the body's ability to digest, absorb and use these nutrients.

Overnourishment. Food intake that is continuously in excess of dietary energy requirements.

Overnutrition. A result of excessive food intake relative to dietary nutrient requirements.

Overweight and obesity. Body weight that is above normal for height as a result of an excessive accumulation of fat. It is usually a manifestation of overnourishment. Overweight is defined as a BMI of more than 25 but less than 30 and obesity as a BMI of 30 or more.

Stunting. Low height for age, reflecting a past episode or episodes of sustained undernutrition.

Undernourishment. A state, lasting for at least one year, of inability to acquire enough food, defined as a level of food intake insufficient to meet dietary energy requirements. For the purposes of this report, hunger was defined as being synonymous with chronic undernourishment.

Undernutrition. The outcome of undernourishment, and/or poor absorption and/or poor biological use of nutrients consumed as a result of repeated infectious disease. It includes being underweight for one's age, too short for one's age (stunted), dangerously thin for one's height (wasted) and deficient in vitamins and minerals (micronutrient malnutrition).

Underweight. Low weight for age in children, and BMI of less than 18.5 in adults, reflecting a current condition resulting from inadequate food intake, past episodes of undernutrition or poor health conditions.

Wasting. Low weight for height, generally the result of weight loss associated with a recent period of starvation or disease.

NOTES

1 The proportion of undernourished people in the total population is the indicator known as prevalence of undernourishment (PoU). See Annexes 2 and 3 of this report for further details.

2 Reference is made here to the developing regions as defined by the M49 country classification of the United Nations (see http://unstats.un.org/unsd/methods/m49/m49regin.htm). Countries included in these regions are also reported in Annex 1, Table A1.

3 If China and India are excluded from the aggregate of the developing regions, the reduction in undernourishment follows a more stable, continuous downward trend. China and India alone account for 81 percent of the total reduction of the number of undernourished people in the developing regions between 1990–92 and 2014–16, and China alone accounts for almost two-thirds.

4 Rome Declaration on World Food Security, adopted at the World Food Summit, Rome, 13–17 November 1996.

5 This is known as target 1c of Millennium Development Goal 1 (MDG 1) (see http://www.un.org/millenniumgoals/).

6 See Annex 2 for details on calculating progress *vis-à-vis* target 1c of MDG 1 and the 1996 WFS goal. The assessment of progress towards these targets, started by FAO at the end of the 1990s, took 1990–92 as the base period. Both the WFS and MDG hunger targets are to be reached by the end of 2015. To maintain consistency, progress has been assessed with reference to a three-year average centred on 2015, that is, 2014–16. Achievement of the MDGs are meant to be assessed for the 25-year period, from 1990 to 2015, but, as observations are only available for the 24-year period from 1990–92 to 2014–16, the 50 percent change required for reaching the targets has had to be adjusted by a factor of 24/25. This corresponds to a 48 percent reduction of the PoU with respect to 1990–92.

7 The share of sub-Saharan Africa increased from 45 percent to over 60 percent.

8 This is the case if the region is considered without Sudan, which was recently added to the Northern Africa subregion after the partition of the country when South Sudan became an independent state in 2011.

9 See note 6 and Annex 2 for details of the assessment of countries that reached the MDG 1c and WFS targets.

10 This is the region called "Middle Africa" in the M49 country classification adopted by the United Nations http://unstats.un.org/unsd/methods/m49/m49regin.htm for the full listing) and Table A1 in Annex 1.

11 Current annual growth rates are, for instance, 2.5 percent in the Gambia and Ghana; 2.6 percent in Mauritania and Togo; 2.7 percent in Benin and Cameroon; 2.9 percent in Malawi, Mali, Mozambique, Nigeria and Sao Tome and Principe; and 3.2 percent in Angola. See Population Reference Bureau. 2014. *World Population Data Sheet 2014* (available at http://www.prb.org/Publications/Datasheets/2014/2014-world-population-data-sheet/data-sheet.aspx).

12 Following the split of former Sudan into two countries in 2011, South Sudan was classified as part of sub-Saharan Africa, while Sudan was added to Northern Africa. In order to allow appropriate assessments of progress between 1990–92 and 2014–16, Sudan is not considered in the Northern Africa region as reported in Figure 4 and Table A1 in Annex 1.

13 See, for example, the case study on Tajikistan in the 2013 edition of this report.

14 See, for example, the case study on Yemen in the 2014 issue of this report.

15 FAO/ECLAC/ALADI. 2015. *The CELAC Plan for Food and Nutrition Security and the Eradication of Hunger 2025*. Executive summary (available at http://www.fao.org/fileadmin/user_upload/rlc/docs/celac/ENG_Plan_CELAC_2025.pdf).

16 See, for example, the case study on Haiti in the 2014 issue of this report.

17 Cyclone Pam with 270 km/hour winds, hit Vanuatu as a category 5 cyclone, the second strongest ever to have formed in the Southern Pacific region.

18 One obvious methodological difference between the two indicators is the population coverage: underweight is measured only for children below five years of age, while undernourishment is measured for the entire population. Other differences relate to the way indicators are compiled. The height and weight of children are directly measured in household surveys, while the availability of and access to sufficient food are estimated using a statistical model that draws from multiple data sources (see Annex 2).

19 The starting point for monitoring the CU5 was the year 1990, whereas it was 1990–92 for the PoU. The last available data point for CU5 is 2013, whereas for the PoU it is 2014–16. Information for the PoU and the CU5 is not available for the same sets of countries. All comparisons are therefore limited to regional aggregates.

20 The Human Development Index was 0.399 in sub-Saharan Africa in 1990, compared with a world average of 0.597. See UNDP. 2014. *Human Development Report 2014. Sustaining human progress. reducing vulnerabilities and building resilience*. New York, USA, Table 2 (available at http://hdr.undp.org/en/content/table-2-human-development-index-trends-1980-2013).

21 The share of GDP devoted to health expenditure in sub-Saharan Africa was three percentage points lower than for the world (6 percent versus 9 percent).

22 For a summary of the debate on this point see N. Alexandratos and J. Bruinsma. 2012. *World agriculture towards 2030/2050: the 2012 revision*. ESA Working paper No. 12-03. Rome, FAO.

23 See, FAO. 2015. *Food security indicators*. Web page (available at http://www.fao.org/economic/ess/ess-fs/ess-fadata/it/#.VRuyjOEZbqc).

24 P. Karfakis, G. Rapsomanikis and E. Scambelloni. 2015 (forthcoming). *The drivers of hunger reduction*. ESA Working Paper. Rome, FAO.

25 Commission on Growth and Development. 2008. *The growth report: strategies for sustained growth and inclusive development*. Washington, DC. World Bank.

26 For a definition of protracted crises, see FAO and WFP. 2010. *The State of Food Insecurity in the World 2010. Addressing food security in protracted crises*. Rome, FAO.

27 See The Geneva Declaration on Armed Violence and Development. 2011. *Global Burden of Armed Violence 2011: lethal encounters*. Geneva, Switzerland (http://www.genevadeclaration.org/measurability/global-burden-of-armed-violence/global-burden-of-armed-violence-2011.html); and FAO. 2013. *Study suggests 258 000 Somalis died due to severe food insecurity and famine*. News release (available at http://www.fao.org/somalia/news/detail-events/en/c/247642/).

28 J.P. Azevedo, G. Inchauste and V. Sanfelice. 2013. *Decomposing the recent inequality decline in Latin America*. Policy Research Working Paper 6715. Washington, DC, World Bank.

29 FAO, IFAD and WFP. 2012. *The State of Food Insecurity in the World 2012. Economic growth is necessary but not sufficient to accelerate reduction of hunger and malnutrition*. Rome, FAO.

30 International Labour Organization (ILO). 2012. *Global Employment Trends 2012. Preventing a deeper job crisis*. Geneva, Switzerland.

31 FAO. 2012. *Decent rural employment for food security: a case for action*. Rome.

32 FAO, IFAD and WFP, 2012 (see note 29) and L. Christiaensen, L. Demery and J. Kuhl. 2011. The (evolving) role of agriculture in poverty reduction: an empirical perspective. *Journal of Development Economics*, 96: 239–254.

33 FAO. 2011. *State of Food and Agriculture 2010–11. Women in agriculture: closing the gender gap for development*. Rome.

34 N. Kabeer. 2014. *Gender equality and economic growth: a view from below*. Paper prepared for UN Women Expert Group Meeting "Envisioning women's rights in the post-2015 context", New York, 3–5 November 2014.

35 International Policy Centre for Inclusive Growth. 2009. *What explains the decline in Brazil's inequality?* One Pager No. 89. Brasilia, International Policy Centre for Inclusive Growth, Poverty Practice, Bureau for Development Policy, United Nations Development Programme and the Government of Brazil.

36 Government of Brazil. 2014. *Indicadores de Desenvolvimento Brasileiro 2001–2012*. Brasilia.

37 FAO. 2014. *The State of Food and Agriculture 2014. Innovation in family farming*. Rome.

38 The calculations are based on data collected from the Global Yield Gap Atlas, an initiative by the University of Nebraska-Lincoln, Wageningen University and Water for Food (see http://www.yieldgap.org/).

39 World Bank. 2008. *World Development Report 2008. Agriculture for development*. Washington, DC; and IFAD. 2011. *Rural Poverty Report 2011. New realities, new challenges: new opportunities for tomorrow's generation*. Rome.

40 H. Thomas, ed. 2006. *Trade reforms and food security: country case studies and synthesis*. Rome, FAO.

41 WomenWatch. 2011. *Gender equality and trade policy*. Resource paper (available at http://www.un.org/womenwatch/feature/trade/gender_equality_and_trade_policy.pdf).

42 E. Magrini, P. Montalbano, S. Nenci and L. Salvatici. 2014. *Agricultural trade policies and food security: is there a causal relationship?* FOODSECURE Working Paper No. 25 (available at http://www3.lei.wur.nl/FoodSecurePublications/25_Salvatici_et_al_Agtrade-policies-FNS.pdf).

43 FAO. 2014. *Policy responses to high food prices in Latin America and the Caribbean: country case studies*, edited by D.Dawe and E. Krivonos. Rome.

44 ILO. 2014. *World Social Protection Report 2014/15. Building economic recovery, inclusive development and social justice*. Geneva, Switzerland.

45 *Ibid*.

46 International Social Security Association. 2011. *Africa: a new balance for social security*. Geneva, Switzerland.

47 U. Gentilini, M. Honorati, and R. Yemtsov. 2014. *The State of Social Safety Nets 2014*. Washington, DC, World Bank.

48 International Labour Conference. 2012. Recommendation no. 202 concerning national floors for social protection (available at http://www.ilo.org/brussels/WCMS_183640/lang--en/index.htm).

49 ILO, 2014 (see note 51).

50 A. Fiszbein, R. Kanbur and R. Yemtsov. 2014. Social protection and poverty reduction: global patterns and some targets. *World Development*, 61(1): 167–177.

51 WFP. 2012. *Bangladesh food security for the ultra poor: lessons learned report 2012*. Rome.

52 M. Madajewicz, A.H. Tsegay and M. Norton. 2013. *Managing risks to agricultural livelihoods: impact evaluation of the HARITA Program in Tigray, Ethiopia, 2009–2012*. Boston, USA, Oxfam America; and FAO. 2014. *The economic impacts of cash transfer programmes in sub-Saharan Africa*. From Protection to Production Policy Brief (available at http://www.fao.org/3/a-i4194e.pdf).

53 *The Lancet*. 2013. Maternal and Child Nutrition series. *The Lancet*, 382(9890); and The Transfer Project. 2015. *The broad range of cash transfer impacts in sub-Saharan Africa: consumption, human capital and productive activity*. Research brief (available at http://ovcsupport.net/wp-content/uploads/2015/03/TP-Broad-Impacts-of-SCT-in-SSA_NOV-2014.pdf).

54 See, for instance, M. Van den Bold, A. Quisumbing and S. Gillespie. *Women's empowerment and nutrition*. IFPRI Discussion Paper No. 01294. Washington, DC, International Food Policy Research Institute.

55 H. Alderman and M. Mustafa. 2013. *Social protection and nutrition*. Note prepared for the Technical Preparatory Meeting for the International Conference on Nutrition (ICN2), Rome, 13–15 November 2013. Rome, FAO and World Health Organization.

56 A. Harmer and J. Macrae, eds. 2004. *Beyond the continuum: aid policy in protracted crises*. HPG Report No.18, p. 1. London, Overseas Development Institute.

57 Criteria for identifying countries in protracted crises: (i) longevity of crisis – at least eight of the past ten years on the Global Information and Early Warning System (GIEWS) list; (ii) aid flows – at least 10 percent of total official development assistance received in the form of humanitarian assistance (between 2000 and 2010); (iii) economic and food security status – countries appear on the list of low-income food-deficit countries. It should be recognized that the methodology employed in *The State of Food Security in the World 2010* (see note 26) used three of a number of possible criteria, and that the list therein is not definitive.

58 The updated list of countries in protracted crisis includes: Afghanistan, Burundi, Central African Republic, Chad, Congo, Cote d'Ivoire, Democratic People's Republic of Korea, Democratic Republic of the Congo, Eritrea, Ethiopia, Guinea, Haiti, Iraq, Kenya, Liberia, Sierra Leone, Somalia, Sudan, Uganda and Zimbabwe.

59 P. Pingali, L. Alinovi and J. Sutton. 2005. Food security in complex emergencies: enhancing food system resilience. *Disasters*, 29(51): S5–S24.

60 High-Level Expert Forum. 2012. *Food insecurity in protracted crises – an overview*. Brief prepared for the High Level Expert Forum on Food Insecurity in Protracted Crises, Rome, 13–14 September 2012.

NOTES

N O T E S

61 Global Information and Early Warning System (GIEWS) list of Countries Requiring External Assistance (available at http://www.fao.org/Giews/english/hotspots/index.htm).

62 Work is ongoing to agree a new compact on how to more effectively manage risk in recurrent and protracted crises, known as the Bosphorus Compact. The compact is expected to be launched in May 2016 at the World Humanitarian Summit.

63 GIEWS list (see note 61).

64 J. Adoko and S. Levine. 2004. *Land matters in displacement: the importance of land rights in Acholiland and what threatens them.* Kampala, Civil Society Organizations for Peace in Northern Uganda.

65 United Nations Develoment Programme (UNDP). 2012. *Africa Human Development Report 2012. Towards a food secure future.* New York, USA.

66 FAO and WFP, 2010 (see note 26).

67 FAO. 1996. *The Sixth World Food Survey.* Rome.

68 C. Cafiero. 2012. Advances in hunger measurement. Presentation at the International Scientific Symposium on Food and Nutrition Security Information: from Valid Measurement to Effective Decision-Making. Rome, FAO Headquarters, 17–19 January 2012.

69 N. Wanner, C. Cafiero, N. Troubat and P. Conforti. 2014. *Refinements to the FAO Methodology for estimating the Prevalence of Undernourishment Indicator.* FAO Statistics Division Working Paper Series ESS / 14-05 (available at http://www.fao.org/3/a-i4046e.pdf).

70 National household surveys include household income and expenditure surveys (HIES), household budget surveys (HBS) and living standard measurement studies (LSMS).

71 J. Gustavsson, C. Cederberg, U. Sonesson, R. van Otterdijk and A. Meybeck. 2011. *Global food losses and food waste: Extent, causes and prevention.* Rome, FAO.

72 Food balance sheet data are available up to the year 2013 for Afghanistan, Algeria, Angola, Bangladesh, Belize, Brazil, Burkina Faso, Chad, China, Colombia, Côte d'Ivoire, Democratic People's Republic of Korea, Dominican Republic, Ethiopia, Guatemala, Haiti, India, Indonesia, Jamaica, Kenya, Madagascar, Mexico, Mozambique, Myanmar, Nepal, Nigeria, Pakistan, Panama, Paraguay, Peru, Philippines, Sri Lanka, Sudan, Thailand, United Republic of Tanzania, Viet Nam, Yemen, Zambia and Zimbabwe. These countries account for about 70 percent of the undernourished people reported in *The State of Food Insecurity in the World 2014.*

73 For more details, see N. Wanner, C. Cafiero, N. Troubat and P. Conforti. 2014. *Refinements to the FAO methodology for estimating the prevalence of undernourishment indicator.* FAO Statistics Division Working Paper No. 14-05. Rome, FAO.

74 T.-H. Kim and H. White. 2004. On more robust estimation of skewness and kurtosis. *Finance Research Letters,* 1(1): 56–73.

75 FAO. 2003. *Proceedings: Measurement and Assessment of Food Deprivation and Undernutrition: International Scientific Symposium, Rome, 26–28 June 2002.* Rome.

76 L.C. Smith. 1998. Can FAO's measure of chronic undernourishment be strengthened? *Food Policy,* 23(5): 425–445.

77 World Bank. 2008. 2005 International *Comparison Program: tables of final results.* Washington, DC.

78 FAOSTAT Statistical database (available at http://faostat.fao.org/).

79 World Bank. All the Ginis database (available at http://econ.worldbank.org/projects/inequality).

80 F. Solt. 2009. Standardizing the world income inequality database. *Social Science Quarterly,* 90(2): 231–242.

81 United Nations. 2013. *World Population Ageing 2013.* New York, USA.

82 United Nations University, WHO and FAO. 2004. *Human energy requirements: Report of a Joint FAO/WHO/UNU Expert Consultation. Rome, 17–24 October 2001.* FAO Food and Nutrition Technical Report Series No. 1. Rome, FAO.

83 United Nations Department of Economic and Social Affairs, Population Division website (available at http://www.un.org/en/development/desa/population/).

84 L. Naiken. 2007. *The probability distribution framework for estimating the prevalence of undernourishment: exploding the myth of the bivariate distribution.* FAO Statistics Division Working Paper No. ESS/ESSG/009e. Rome, FAO.

85 A. Deaton and J. Drèze. 2009. Food and nutrition in India: facts and interpretations. *Economic and Political Weekly,* XLIV(7): 42–65.

86 P. Svedberg. 1999. 841 million undernourished? *World Development,* 27(12): 2081–2098.

87 Committee on World Food Security. 2001. *The World Food Summit Goal and the Millennium Development Goals.* CFS: 2001/2-Sup.1, Twenty-seventh Session, Rome, 28 May–1 June 2001. Rome.

88 Rome Declaration on World Food Security (see note 4).

Notes for Annex 1

Countries revise their official statistics regularly for the past as well as the latest reported period. The same holds for population data of the United Nations. Whenever this happens, FAO revises its estimates of undernourishment accordingly. Therefore, users are advised to refer to changes in estimates over time only within the same edition of *The State of Food Insecurity in the World* and refrain from comparing data published in editions for different years.

Countries, areas and territories for which there were insufficient or not reliable data to conduct the assessment are not reported. These include: American Samoa, Andorra, Anguilla, Aruba, Bahrain, Bhutan, British Virgin Islands, Burundi, Canton and Enderbury Islands, Cayman Islands, Christmas Island, Cocos (Keeling) Islands, Cook Islands, Comoros, Democratic Republic of the Congo, Dominica, Equatorial Guinea, Eritrea, Faeroe Islands, French Guiana, French Polynesia, Greenland, Guadeloupe, Guam, Holy See, Johnston Island, Libya, Liechtenstein, Marshall Islands, Martinique, Micronesia (Federated States of), Midway Islands, Monaco, Nauru, Netherlands Antilles, New Caledonia, Niue, Norfolk Island, Northern Mariana Islands, Palau, Papua New Guinea, Pitcairn Islands, Puerto Rico, Qatar, Réunion, Saint Helena, Saint Pierre and Miquelon, Saint Kitts and Nevis, San Marino, Seychelles, Singapore, Somalia, Syrian Arab Republic, Tokelau, Tonga, Turks and Caicos Islands, Tuvalu, United States Virgin Islands, Wake Island, Wallis and Futuna Islands, Western Sahara.

. World Food Summit goal: halve, between 1990–92 and 2015, the number of people undernourished.

. Millennium Development Goal 1, target 1c: halve, between 1990–92 and 2015, the proportion of people suffering from undernourishment, or reduce this proportion below 5 percent. Indicator 1.9 measures the proportion of the population below the minimum level of dietary energy consumption (undernourishment). The results are obtained following a harmonized methodology and are based on the latest globally available data averaged over three years. Some countries may have more recent data which, if used, could lead to different estimates of the prevalence of undernourishment and consequently of the progress achieved.

. Projection.

. Change from the 1990–92 baseline. For countries that did not exist in the baseline period, the 1990–92 proportion of undernourished is based on the 1993–95 proportion, while the number of people undernourished is based on this proportion of their 1990–92 population. For countries where the prevalence of undernourishment is estimated to be below 5 percent, the change in the number of people undernourished since the 1990–92 baseline is only assessed as: achieving the WFS target, i.e. reducing the number by more than half (<−50.0%); progress, but insufficient to achieve the WFS target, i.e. reducing the number by less than half (>−50.0%); or an increase in the number of people undernourished (>0.0%).

. The colour indicator shows the progress achieved by 2014–16:

WFS target		MDG target	
▲	WFS target not achieved, with lack of progress or deterioration	🔴	MDG target 1c not achieved, with lack of progress or deterioration
◀▶	WFS target not achieved, with slow progress	🟡	MDG target 1c not achieved, with slow progress
▼	WFS target close to being achieved. Will be achieved before 2020 if observed trend persists	⭕	MDG target 1c close to being achieved. Will be achieved before 2020 if observed trend persists
✳	WFS target achieved	🟢	MDG target 1c achieved

Country composition of the special groupings:

. Includes: Afghanistan, Angola, Bangladesh, Benin, Burkina Faso, Burundi, Cambodia, Central African Republic, Chad, Comoros, Democratic Republic of the Congo, Djibouti, Eritrea, Ethiopia, Gambia, Guinea, Guinea-Bissau, Haiti, Kiribati, Lao People's Democratic Republic, Lesotho, Liberia, Madagascar, Malawi, Mali, Mauritania, Mozambique, Myanmar, Nepal, Niger, Rwanda, Sao Tome and Principe, Senegal, Sierra Leone, Solomon Islands, Somalia, Sudan, Timor-Leste, Togo, Uganda, United Republic of Tanzania, Vanuatu, Yemen, Zambia.

. Includes: Afghanistan, Armenia, Azerbaijan, Bolivia (Plurinational State of), Botswana, Burkina Faso, Burundi, Central African Republic, Chad, Ethiopia, Kazakhstan, Kyrgyzstan, Lao People's Democratic Republic, Lesotho, Malawi, Mali, Mongolia, Nepal, Niger, Paraguay, Republic of Moldova, Rwanda, Swaziland, Tajikistan, Turkmenistan, Uganda, The former Yugoslav Republic of Macedonia, Uzbekistan, Zambia, Zimbabwe.

. Includes: Antigua and Barbuda, Bahamas, Barbados, Belize, Cabo Verde, Comoros, Cuba, Dominica, Dominican Republic, Fiji Islands, Grenada, Guinea-Bissau, Guyana, Haiti, Jamaica, Kiribati, Maldives, Mauritius, Netherlands Antilles, New Caledonia, Papua New Guinea, Saint Kitts and Nevis, Saint Lucia, Saint Vincent and the Grenadines, Samoa, Sao Tome and Principe, Seychelles, Solomon Islands, Suriname, Timor-Leste, Trinidad and Tobago, Vanuatu.

. Includes: Afghanistan, Bangladesh, Benin, Burkina Faso, Burundi, Cambodia, Central African Republic, Chad, Comoros, Democratic People's Republic of Korea, Democratic Republic of the Congo, Eritrea, Ethiopia, Gambia, Guinea, Guinea-Bissau, Haiti, Kenya, Liberia, Madagascar, Malawi, Mali, Mozambique, Myanmar, Nepal, Niger, Rwanda, Sierra Leone, Somalia, Tajikistan, Togo, Uganda, United Republic of Tanzania, Zimbabwe.

10. Includes: Armenia, Bolivia (Plurinational State of), Cameroon, Cabo Verde, Congo, Côte d'Ivoire, Djibouti, Egypt, El Salvador, Georgia, Ghana, Guatemala, Guyana, Honduras, India, Indonesia, Kiribati, Kosovo, Kyrgyzstan, Lao People's Democratic Republic, Lesotho, Mauritania, Mongolia, Morocco, Nicaragua, Nigeria, Pakistan, Papua New Guinea, Paraguay, Philippines, Republic of Moldova, Samoa, Sao Tome and Principe, Senegal, Solomon Islands, South Sudan, Sri Lanka, Sudan, Swaziland, Syrian Arab Republic, Timor-Leste, Ukraine, Uzbekistan, Vanuatu, Viet Nam, West Bank and Gaza Strip, Yemen, Zambia.

11. Includes: Afghanistan, Bangladesh, Benin, Burkina Faso, Burundi, Cameroon, Central African Republic, Chad, Comoros, Congo, Côte d'Ivoire, Democratic People's Republic of Korea, Democratic Republic of the Congo, Djibouti, Eritrea, Ethiopia, Gambia, Ghana, Guinea, Guinea-Bissau, Haiti, Honduras, India, Kenya, Kyrgyzstan, Lesotho, Liberia, Madagascar, Malawi, Mali, Mauritania, Mongolia, Mozambique, Nepal, Nicaragua, Niger, Nigeria, Papua New Guinea, Philippines, Rwanda, Sao Tome and Principe, Senegal, Sierra Leone, Solomon Islands, Somalia, Sri Lanka, Sudan, Tajikistan, Togo, Uganda, United Republic of Tanzania, Uzbekistan, Yemen, Zimbabwe.

12. "Africa" includes developing countries falling under the responsibility of the FAO Regional Office RAF: Angola, Benin, Botswana, Burkina Faso, Burundi, Cameroon, Cabo Verde, Central African Republic, Chad, Comoros, Congo, Côte d'Ivoire, Democratic Republic of the Congo, Djibouti, Eritrea, Ethiopia, Gabon, Gambia, Ghana, Guinea, Guinea-Bissau, Kenya, Lesotho, Liberia, Madagascar, Malawi, Mali, Mauritania, Mauritius, Mozambique, Namibia, Niger, Nigeria, Rwanda, Sao Tome and Principe, Senegal, Seychelles, Sierra Leone, Somalia, South Africa, Sudan (former) (up to 2011), South Sudan (from 2012), Swaziland, Togo, Uganda, United Republic of Tanzania, Zambia, Zimbabwe.

13. "Asia and the Pacific" includes developing countries falling under the responsibility of the FAO Regional Office RAP: Afghanistan, Bangladesh, Bhutan, Brunei Darussalam, Cambodia, China, Democratic People's Republic of Korea, Fiji, India, Indonesia, Iran (Islamic Republic of), Kazakhstan, Kiribati, Lao People's Democratic Republic, Malaysia, Maldives, Mongolia, Myanmar, Nepal, Pakistan, Papua New Guinea, Philippines, Republic of Korea, Samoa, Singapore, Solomon Islands, Sri Lanka, Thailand, Timor-Leste, Uzbekistan, Vanuatu, Viet Nam.

14. "Europe and Central Asia" includes developing countries falling under the responsibility of the FAO Regional Office REU: Armenia, Azerbaijan, Georgia, Kazakhstan, Kyrgyzstan, Tajikistan, Turkey, Turkmenistan, Uzbekistan.

15. "Latin America and the Caribbean" includes developing countries falling under the responsibility of the FAO Regional Office RLC: Antigua and Barbuda, Argentina, Bahamas, Barbados, Belize, Bolivia (Plurinational state of), Brazil, Chile, Colombia, Costa Rica, Cuba, Dominica, Dominican Republic, Ecuador, El Salvador, Grenada, Guatemala, Guyana, Haiti, Honduras, Jamaica, Mexico, Nicaragua, Panama, Paraguay, Peru, Saint Kitts and Nevis, Saint Lucia, Saint Vincent and the Grenadines, Suriname, Trinidad and Tobago, Uruguay, Venezuela (Bolivarian Republic of).

16. "Near East and North Africa" includes developing countries falling under the responsibility of the FAO Regional Office RNE: Algeria, Egypt, Iran (Islamic Republic of), Iraq, Jordan, Kuwait, Lebanon, Libya, Mauritania, Morocco, Saudi Arabia, Sudan (from 2012), Syrian Arab Republic, Tunisia, United Arab Emirates, Yemen.

17. Excludes Sudan. In addition to the countries listed in the table, includes Libya.

18. In addition to the countries listed in the table, includes: Burundi, Comoros, Democratic Republic of the Congo, Eritrea, Seychelles, Somalia. The value for 2014–16 includes an estimate for South Sudan.

19. Sudan (former) refers to the former sovereign state of Sudan prior to July 2011, when South Sudan declared its independence. Data for South Sudan and Sudan for the years 2014–16 are not reliable and are not reported.

20. In addition to the countries listed in the table, includes: Syrian Arab Republic, West Bank and Gaza Strip.

21. In addition to the countries listed in the table, includes: Antigua and Barbuda, Bahamas, Dominica, Grenada, Saint Kitts and Nevis, Saint Lucia, Netherlands Antilles.

22. In addition to the countries listed in the table includes: French Polynesia, New Caledonia, Papua New Guinea. Australia and New Zealand are considered in the "developed countries" group.

KEY

<5.0   proportion of undernourished less than 5 percent

<0.1   less than 100 000 people undernourished

na   not applicable

ns   not statistically significant

Source: FAO estimates.

Key messages

- About 795 million people are undernourished globally, down 167 million over the last decade, and 216 million less than in 1990–92. The decline is more pronounced in developing regions, despite significant population growth. In recent years, progress has been hindered by slower and less inclusive economic growth as well as political instability in some developing regions, such as Central Africa and western Asia.

- The year 2015 marks the end of the monitoring period for the Millennium Development Goal targets. For the developing regions as a whole, the share of undernourished people in the total population has decreased from 23.3 percent in 1990–92 to 12.9 per cent. Some regions, such as Latin America, the east and south-eastern regions of Asia, the Caucasus and Central Asia, and the northern and western regions of Africa have made fast progress. Progress was also recorded in southern Asia, Oceania, the Caribbean and southern and eastern Africa, but at too slow a pace to reach the MDG 1c target of halving the proportion of the chronically undernourished.

- A total of 72 developing countries out of 129, or more than half the countries monitored, have reached the MDG 1c hunger target. Most enjoyed stable political conditions and economic growth, often accompanied by social protection policies targeted at vulnerable population groups.

- For the developing regions as a whole, the two indicators of MDG 1c – the prevalence of undernourishment and the proportion of underweight children under 5 years of age – have both declined. In some regions, including western Africa, south-eastern Asia and South America, undernourishment declined faster than the rate for child underweight, suggesting room for improving the quality of diets, hygiene conditions and access to clean water, particularly for poorer population groups.

- Economic growth is a key success factor for reducing undernourishment, but it has to be inclusive and provide opportunities for improving the livelihoods of the poor. Enhancing the productivity and incomes of smallholder family farmers is key to progress.

- Social protection systems have been critical in fostering progress towards the MDG 1 hunger and poverty targets in a number of developing countries. Social protection directly contributes to the reduction of poverty, hunger and malnutrition by promoting income security and access to better nutrition, health care and education. By improving human capacities and mitigating the impacts of shocks, social protection fosters the ability of the poor to participate in growth through better access to employment.

- In many countries that have failed to reach the international hunger targets, natural and human-induced disasters or political instability have resulted in protracted crises with increased vulnerability and food insecurity of large parts of the population. In such contexts, measures to protect vulnerable population groups and improve livelihoods have been difficult to implement or ineffective.

FAO information products are available on the FAO website (www.fao.org/publications) and can be purchased through publications-sales@fao.org

www.ingramcontent.com/pod-product-compliance
Lightning Source LLC
Chambersburg PA
CBHW060828270326
41931CB00003B/105